barking

barking

joe bennett

HAZARD PRESS
publishers

All articles in this book were first published in the
Christchurch *Press*, the Wellington *DominionPost*,
the *New Zealand Herald*, *Hawkes Bay Today*,
the *Otago Daily Times*, the *Waikato Times*
or the *Southland Times*.

First published 2003
© 2003 Joe Bennett

ISBN 1-877270-49-0

Published by Hazard Press
P.O. Box 2151, Christchurch, New Zealand
Front cover photograph by John McCombe
Cover design by Working Ideas
Printed in New Zealand

Contents

Lotsdeadredindians 8

A long way away 11

Big cherub 14

Land you can play with 17

If coxes go 20

Captain Sensible and co. 23

Jules 26

Dreams on wheels 29

All squared away 32

Giggle and bleed 35

Lovers by pen and gum 38

At two drunks swimming 41

Dawn ducks 44

For our convenience 47

Not quite death in the afternoon 50

Girlie sox 53

Cheap and stationary 56

His favourite word is and 59

Go and eat sky 62

Put that head back 65

Food, fun and a tickle behind the ear 68

Oi Popey-boy 71

Shock revelations 74

Oooh la bloody la 77

Wrong room 80

Paper faith 83

Sorry about the stains 86

Artistes and Belgians   89
Into a briar bush   92
The juiciness   95
And let him hate you   98
Hope is dead   101
In and out   104
Unreal   107
Exactly, yes, me too   110
Is there anybody there?   113
No children litter the step   116
Yes, coach   119
He was my English teacher   122
Hacksaw that shackle   125
Hot wet air   128
A coupette   131
Easter rising   134

Foreword

George Orwell said that every writer was both vain and lazy. Assuming a columnist counts as a writer, then I'm with him. Every word I write is a victory for vanity over laziness. Every unwritten word's a defeat.

Orwell also said that every writer was to some degree an aesthete. I'm with him on that too. Sweet language tempts me to believe things I don't believe and to say things I don't mean.

He was a wise fellow, old George, but he was terribly serious. I'm not with him on that.

J.B.
Lyttelton, May 2003

Lotsadeadredindians

Nicols Fox has written a book called *Against the Machine* in which she puts the case against labour-saving domestic gadgets.

Some years ago her clothes-drier broke down and she was forced to peg clothes on a line. 'I discovered that the trip outside to the clothesline forced me to interact with the day in a new way . . . Now I hang clothes outside every day, even in the Maine winter.'

Ms Fox is especially harsh on dishwashers. She recalls her idyllic childhood in backwoods America – I forget the actual name of the place but Lotsadeadredindians will do – where 'my mother and grandmother and I used to wash the dishes together in the kitchen and we had a lot of really good conversations in the process. They passed along stories and lessons for life . . . washing dishes wasn't just washing dishes. It was a kind of event.'

For Ms Fox, the dishwasher not only discourages such inter-generational exchange but also 'robs you of the only interesting aspect of dishwashing which is how to get off that piece of cheese that's stuck to the plate'.

A bestseller in paperback, *Against the Machine* has now been made into a play. And in a scoop I present the first scene.

Location – a kitchen in a log cabin in Lotsadeadredindians.

Cast – Nicols Fox as a girl and Grandma Bristlechin.

Action – the dishes.

Grandma Bristlechin: Why look you here, my child.

Nicols: What is it, Grandmama?

Grandma Bristlechin: Just you look at that. Oh me oh my, if that ain't the most interesting piece of cheese I've seen stuck to a plate in many a long year I'll eat the rim off my stetson and boil the rest of it into an apple-pie for Thanksgiving.

Nicols: Grandmama, can I ask you a question in the interests of pursuing an intergenerational conversation?

Grandma Bristlechin: You go right ahead, my child, while I gets a-scraping with this here knuckle bone that's somehow become exposed through 103 years of washing dishes.

Nicols: What's menstruation?

Pause.

Nicols: Grandmama?

Grandma Bristlechin: What is it, my li'l potato dumpling?

Nicols: I asked you an intergenerational question in order to give you the opportunity to pass on a story or a lesson for life and you didn't say nothing, Grandmama.

Grandma Bristlechin: Well, bless me, my child. I guess I just got too carried away with this here interesting morsel of cheese.

Nicols: Grandmama, why was I given such a ridiculous Christian name?

Grandma Bristlechin: My, you're full of questions for a li'l girl. Any fuller and your freckles'll pop off and your dungarees bust and that's not something should happen afore the apples are safely in the barn and . . .

Nicols: Is this a story or a lesson for life, Grandmama?

Grandma Bristlechin: There you go again, child. Why not go ask your momma. She's outside at the clothesline interacting with the day.

Nicols: But Grandmama, there's three foot of snow on the ground.

Grandma Bristlechin: Once a woman discovers pegging out there ain't no snowdrift in the whole of Lotsadeadredindians gonna put her off her daily interaction. But maybe by rights you should be fetching her in now afore she comes over all brittle again. *(Exit Nicols.)* Whoa, steady there, my child. What with all that energy of yourn you'll be a-tripping over the chain that's bound me to this sink for 103 years, the chain I do love so much I bless every li'l festering ulcer on my pretty ankle.

(Re-enter Nicols dragging her stiff blue mother whom she props against the dado.)

Nicols: Grandmama, what's a dado?

Grandma Bristlechin: There you go again, asking them questions of yourn. I swear there's more questions in you than there's crackers in that there weevil barrel.

Nicols: It's just the stage directions told me to prop Mother against it.

Grandma Bristlechin: Oh my child, move her this minute or she'll be a-dripping again and drenching the wainscotting.

Nicols (thoughtfully as she moves Mother to the larder): Grandmama, when I grow up I'm going to write a book and I'll become famous and rich and then I'll buy you a dishwasher and . . .

Grandma Bristlechin (snatching up her granddaughter and rubbing her fiercely across her chin until she draws blood): Now there'll be no more of that devil's talk from you, my child, or I'll be washing your mouth out with pork fat and sourdough, do you hear me? Where did you go learning them dirty words like dishwasher from? Why the dishwasher ain't even been invented yet and to tell the truth I ain't rightly sure it should be. Anyway I won't be having none under my roof, nor any of that clothes-drier business I heard you whispering about with young Jack Thimbleshift under the haybarn the other day. I'm onto you my girl, don't you worry.

Nicols wriggles out of Grandma Bristlechin's grasp and runs off stage right defiantly screaming, 'Clothes drier, dishwasher, other labour-saving devices' while Grandma Bristlechin reaches calmly under the sink for her Smith & Wesson .303 and takes careful aim offstage. Curtain. Under the curtain a puddle forms as Momma thaws in time for Scene 2 in which Nicols begins to revise her position on gadgetry.

A long way away

Friday evening in a village in Wiltshire, England. All the buildings are made of stone the colour of dirty honey. The village squats in a river valley just off the A40 and the narrow street is thick with mist. The street lights look like hazy moons. I push through the door of a pub. On the floor a somnolent mongrel raises its head an inch to take me in, then flops back down. At the bar a bald young man. His dark blue tailored shirt with bright white collars and cuffs announces that he deals in money. His ears are tiny. They look as though they may have been burned when young and then surgically refashioned. Their rims are crinkled, like the ridge on a pasty.

I say hello. He answers in the deeply rich self-confident accent that speaks of privilege and private education. Despite myself, I like the voice. It doesn't defer.

He is a private-client sharebroker. He's flying to Hong Kong tomorrow to flog off shares to British plutocrats who live there.

'British shares?' I ask.

He shakes his head and chuckles. 'These are seriously wealthy men,' he says. 'They're not interested in mature markets, especially now. They want new markets where the risks are big, but the potential bigger.'

'Like?' I ask.

'Like Kazakhstan,' he says, then mentions other places that I've heard of only from reports of war or famine.

'I see,' I say. 'So I don't suppose you deal on the New Zealand sharemarket.'

'I didn't know there was one,' he says. He pauses. Then, 'I'm sorry, I hope that wasn't rude. I'd love to go to New Zealand. I've seen *Lord of the Rings*.'

Sunday lunchtime. A pub in Greek Street, Soho, central London and two old men at the bar. One is grizzled but dressed in a suit, smoking cigarettes and drinking pints of bitter. The other's dressed as if for racing at Ascot – wing collar, bow-tie, an extravagant silk handkerchief cascading from his breast pocket, and cufflinks the size of military medals. He drinks gin and smokes a cigar an inch in diameter. As I sit down I catch the end of a conversation.

'He told me,' says the man with cufflinks, 'he doesn't want to live to be eighty.'

'He will when he's seventy-nine,' says the other.

The two men never look at each other. They stare across the bar at the optics and the mirrored wall and the sandwiches under a hump of grey perspex. Their conversation seems to be part performance. But the barman and I are the only audience. The barman is dishevelled and Czech.

Both men despise most things and relish saying so. Their conversation ranges over Tony Blair (hollow, hypocritical), the French (perfidious, conniving), death duties, gardening and Mormons. When their bitterness is especially pointed and precise, I laugh. They recognise that I'm listening, that they have drawn me in, but still don't look my way. And then, to my surprise, they talk of rugby.

'Right now,' says the grizzled one, 'England's got the best team in the world.'

'Perhaps,' I say, speaking for the first time, 'but England won't win the World Cup. When it counts, they crumble.'

Though still he doesn't look at me, the grizzled one asks me where I'm from. I tell him.

'Ah,' he says, 'the All Blacks. They used to be all right. But they've gone soft.'

Tuesday evening and a low-beamed pub in rich and wooded Surrey. A woman drinks whisky alone at the bar. She tells the barman about the dog she has adopted that keeps running back to where its former owner lived. The former owner is dead.

When the barman disappears to serve, or to pretend to serve, a customer in the other bar, the woman turns to me. She asks if I know anything of dogs. An hour or so later she gets to speak again and asks me where I'm from.

'Oh,' she says with suddenly bright eyes, 'my youngest son lives in New Zealand. He followed a Kiwi girl and married her. They live in the South Island.'

I tell her that's where I live too.

'Oh,' she exclaims, 'then you must know him', and she tells me his name.

When I shake my head she seems more surprised than disappointed.

And then last Thursday, flying home. The plane en route from Sydney makes landfall over Hokitika. The air is clear and the Southern Alps stand like polished teeth. The English woman next to me, who's been reading a book of French literary theory but has barely turned a page, asks me to point out Mount Cook.

The mountains all look much the same to me. 'There,' I say and I point with a deliberately wobbly finger. Beyond the Alps I can see the glacial lakes of the Mackenzie Basin. They are bluer than sky.

'What day is it?' she asks.

I tell her Thursday.

'I left London on Tuesday,' she says, then pauses. 'I've been flying for ever. New Zealand's a long way away.'

She returns to looking out of the window. 'It's beautiful,' she says, 'I can't see any buildings.'

Big cherub

Sometimes I think of Michael Catt.

I wonder how he is and what he's up to. Whether he's selling real estate or training to be a plumber. Or whether, and this seems to be more likely, he's retired to a cottage in the mountains in some obscure and unvisited country, Lithuania, say, to read books of an escapist nature behind walls topped with razor wire.

Because Michael Catt was the English rugby player who half a dozen years ago was erased by Jonah Lomu. Even if you live in Lapland and smoke fish, even if you're a director of feminist studies, or even if your mind is wandering in a rest home that smells of disinfectant, you will have seen the tape.

The giant Lomu, puffing his cheeks like one of those cherubs in the corners of old maps, bore down on the English try line. He shrugged off tacklers as if they were so many cobwebs. One stood square in his way but succeeded in impeding the giant's momentum to about the same extent as a garden wall impedes a bulldozer. Lomu simply lowered his shoulder, braced his body and then proceeded over the rubble.

And finally in front of him stood Michael Catt, alone on a thin white line. Michael Catt adopted the position, the position they had taught him at school, the crouching position from which you launch a tackle on an oncoming opponent, driving with your legs and placing your head to the side of the body and . . . Lomu simply went both through and over Michael Catt. He chose to inhabit the space that Michael Catt had thought was his, and with the commentator memorably forsaking speech in favour of a series of gasps that shortened and quickened and overtook each other as if he, the commentator, were approaching sexual climax, Lomu scored the try. And in doing so he wrote Michael Catt into the catalogue of memorable images, images that are the common property of the world: Armstrong on the moon, the slumping Kennedy, the man and the tank in Tiananmen Square.

Life today cannot be easy for Michael Catt. In the Lithuanian corner shop the women in headscarves will pause in their perusal of the rollmop herrings and nudge and point and ask each other whether that isn't the poor chap who . . . For Michael Catt exists in the public mind as the frontispiece in Jonah's book of fame. Though an international rugby player in his own right he is known to millions only as the man who fell that another should rise.

Jonah's fans are not primarily rugby players. They are children who like Superman. And at heart we are all children who like Superman. In a decade of rugby Lomu has given us half a dozen glimpses of the human body taken to a new dimension. He's as near as reality has come to the Ubermensch, six-gun Arnie, the Hydra-slaying Hercules, the muscled superhero of the comic strips and a thousand identical video games. Hence the clamouring excited mobs, the mobs in London, the mobs in Paris, the mobs everywhere he goes. He is a myth made flesh. His pneumatic thighs are objects of reverence.

A poor child, from an immigrant underclass, he found success through physique. And now men from the overclass, men in ties, come flocking to hear him speak and to laugh with propitiatory willingness at his jokes. But in truth the men don't come to hear him. They come only to be near him, to be in his presence.

I've never met the man but he seems to be good. So far he has stayed loyal to New Zealand, resisting blandishments no doubt from every country in the world where rugby is played and where there is money. He is rich but he could have been many times richer.

And yet he retains something of his mean-streets heritage. He drives the sort of car I can neither understand nor condone, a low-slung throatmobile, with a boombox in the back that can shatter paving slabs. And he wears a tuft on his shaven head that on anyone else would look silly. On a superhero it looks apt.

There is also something endearing about him. I saw him interviewed some years ago about his clandestine wedding. The interviewer asked him questions in the tone one would use to a child lost in a shopping mall. It was nauseating, intrusive, wrong – and faultless tabloid television. The big man wept. The ad break was delayed as the camera zoomed in on the ratings.

I have heard Lomu called a genius. He is not a genius. Despite ten years of coaching by the best in the land he still passes, catches, kicks and tackles with little more skill than the average club player and he seems to have learnt no new tricks. But when he runs at people, the crowd rise to their feet as one and roar without knowing that they're roaring. They're roaring at a myth on the move. They're roaring for the man in front of him to crumple. They're roaring for another flattened Catt.

Land you can play with

Cold rain drilled the roof all day. I didn't notice when it stopped. Now, mid-evening, my duties done, I am horizontal on the sofa, head propped on a dirty cushion, a fat book on my chest. My dog has wrapped herself twice about the gas fire, singeing her belly-fur. The deep luxurious cocoon of winter.

There seems too much light at the window. I roll off the sofa, push back the blind. Snow. Dropping past the window in big, slow flakes. My heart lifts like a child's heart.

I have never believed that the Eskimos have eighty-seven words for snow. You need only one word. Snow. Listen to it. It sounds like snow.

Snow settles here perhaps twice a decade. It's the guest that visits rarely, surprisingly, and everywhere, in slippers. It takes a known landscape and makes it new.

And you have to be the first to defile it. I can no more resist snow than I can resist the best people. Boots, hat. My dog rises and stretches. She doesn't know what's beyond the door. She has seen snow only once before. A puppy then, she danced and snorted in it, unable to grasp the nature of a world new-made. I open the door and we stand at the threshold of the white world like two children. Like Adam and Eve.

She hesitates, sniffs the snow, advances into it and then we're off up the untouched road. As we climb I turn to look at the black wet marks of my boots and her paws and I think Robinson Crusoe. Then on to the hills.

Snow is land that you can play with. I toss a snowball. It hits a bush and disintegrates. My dog rushes to fetch it and cannot find it. I toss another. She jumps to catch it in the air, bites it and I hear her jaws clash. She sneezes and shakes her head and her body writhes with the game. I toss more and more. She leaps for each one, and bites through it.

The snow falls on my sweater and melts into black. It falls on her fur and stays white until she shakes it off. It is falling in big wet flakes. Further up the hill it forms miniature drifts in the grass. It bends the stems of ragwort, the brushes of broom. Though my hands are numb I cannot resist its texture. I throw snowballs at fenceposts. I strike the branches of trees and then scamper backwards out of the mini-blizzard, shaking myself like a dog.

On the hills deep silence, a giant muffling. I think that I can hear the snowflakes landing. And underfoot the stuff squeaks. Through the cloud the moon shows phosphorescent-oily. The snow won't let the light sink into the land. It tosses it back and gleams. The hills are sharp-edged.

I stop to look down over the white roofs of Lyttelton. I can hear children emerging to squeal and slide and fall and cry. The snow is a better and more unexpected gift than Christmas.

Over a fence and a ridge and then down the side of a silent valley to visit my old dog's grave. I've piled rocks there. I don't disturb their cap of snow. I stand a while. The wet has seeped through my boots, soaked my socks, is starting to numb my toes. I don't much mind. The feeling is as memory-laden as a smell.

The snow has stopped. I urge it to start again. Going back down the hill my boot whips out from under me and I am suddenly heavily on my back. Jarred. Up-ended like a circus clown. Snow's anarchic, a worldwide banana skin. It sends trucks slewing, sends wheels spinning suddenly useless. With heavy slow insistence it breaks our cables, saps our power, defeats us, makes us fools.

I am not hurt. Snow tossed me over but broke my fall. I lie a while. My dog waits with animal patience. At the foot of the path a house. Guests are leaving. The open front door glows golden like a Christmas card. Voices are excited by the snow. 'Be careful now. Be careful.' The snow magnifies the sound, reflects it as it reflects light. I put my dog on the lead. There's a puppyish zest in her.

While we've been up the hill a mass of people have trodden the road, all doing as we've done. The snow is soiled and ruined slush. Past a house where a neighbour sits with his son. They have double glazing, never draw their curtains. They are watching television.

Rain starts to fall, pitting the snow. In the morning it will have gone.

If coxes go

The Apples of Sodom are back. According to *Brewer's Dictionary of Phrase and Fable*, the Apples of Sodom looked lovely but tasted of ashes. They were found on the shores of the Dead Sea. Today they are found in supermarkets.

The supermarket apple looks jake. It is the ad photographer's dream, waxed and buffed and round as a rich red pregnancy. But it tastes, whoa, it tastes as market research has said it ought to taste. It tastes to give no offence. It tastes of sugared water. And not only is it bland as fizzy pop, it is too big. It's big as a buttock.

A true apple is the size of a tennis ball. It fits a fist. But a modern export Fuji would fit a ballista. It would have W. Tell Jr staggering under its weight. Daddy could shoot an arrow through it at a hundred yards with his eyes closed. And drunk. On cider.

Just as shop-window mannequins have no nipples, no pubic hair, no eyes, no dimples of cellulite, no distinction, no sapid pungent life, so modern apples have no warts or cankers, no blemishes. They are giant, parody apples, two of them to the pound.

It was not always so. The apple has a noble history. Was it not an apple that tempted us from paradise? Was it not Adam's richly human lust to sink his young white teeth into the swollen yielding ripeness of an apple that drove a wedge for all eternity between the human race and the immortal verities of God? No it wasn't. There is no apple in Genesis. There is only 'the fruit of the tree in the midst of the garden'.

But we have always called it an apple because the apple is the king and queen and prince of fruits. Other fruit don't come near. Is anyone the mango of your eye? Did Newton find inspiration in a lemon? Does Scandinavian myth embrace the banana of eternal youth?

But there is no need to go back to prehistory. A decade or two is enough. Sturmers, Jonathans, Beefings, Worcesters, Pippins, Russets, Pearmans – in the late summers of my youth they arrived at the greengrocer's in waves. Each came in for a few weeks, ripened from small and green to soft as autumn, then disappeared for another year. The Russet had skin that felt like sandpaper and looked like a disease. But its flesh was sweet as virginity. The Sturmer looked greener than it tasted. The Jonathan, if I remember rightly, was tiger-striped to sweetness and often held a maggot. None of these apples were regular and most were six to the pound.

I have always loved apples, have eaten tons of them, but some twenty years ago I went to North America and there I bit into the future. I met Red Delicious and McIntosh: apples as red as the most mortified blush; apples as polished as furniture; apples as big as grapefruit; apples that tasted like pap.

The world, of course, has followed. The old trees have been torn from the soil and burned. The new breeds have supplanted them and no one could blame the orchardist. The new breeds crop more heavily. They resist blights. They last longer in the cold store and on the shelf. They seduce the shopper's eye. And they have banished seasons. The world is now awash with apples all year round, apples that look lovelier than apples have a right to look, apples I don't want to eat.

But perhaps I am just bleating like a lamb lost on the long mountainside of middle age. Perhaps I am like François Villon who asked, 'Où sont les neiges d'antan?' Which translates, broadly speaking, as 'things ain't what they used to be'.

When we are young everything fizzes. Even boredom fizzes. It is more boring, more intense, more mournful. And that intensity is especially true of the senses. Smells are fiercer, touch more vivid. And taste is brighter, sharper, more seductive. So, perhaps it's not the apples that have waned, but rather my taste-buds, dulled by time and abuse.

No. It is the apples. I know because there remains one true

apple. I await it every year. It is the Cox's Orange Pippin. It comes into the shops when it is hard and green. Avoid it then. Wait a fortnight. Wait till it dents slightly at the squeeze. Then gorge. When I am queuing at the checkout with a bag of ripe Coxes I dribble. I'm dribbling now. If Coxes go, then Sodom.

Captain Sensible and co.

During elections all manner of things shrink. Policies shrink. They become simplistic headlines. Parties shrink. They become their leaders. In some countries even the population shrinks. During the present election in Papua New Guinea about thirty people have died.

Here we had no deaths. Instead we had a resurrection. The corpse was the oh-so-aptly named Mr Dunne. His United Future Party looked like having no party, no future and a unity of one. It was worm tucker. But then the worm administered CPR.

Mr Dunne emerged from the grave looking frankly baffled. He blinked rapidly in the unaccustomed sunlight, groped for an identity and became the champion of common sense. It was a champion move. Common sense is defined as the thing that you've got and others haven't. So a vote for common sense is a vote for yourself. Captain Sensible soared.

Ms Clark's mouth falls naturally into the shape of a coathanger. She's the intellectual giant of our politics, specialising in scorn. Eager to shrug off her dependence on pesky little parties, she called the election in the hope of becoming the only buffalo on the political prairie.

When the pesky little critters tried to nuzzle up to her flanks or nip at them, she turned a cumbrous head and snorted with derision. But in the end she charged only once. Poor John Campbell got it in the groin.

On the buffalo's shoulders perched chirpy Mr Anderton, the harmless pilot bird. Archival footage revealed that he has combed his hair the same way for thirty years. And after those thirty years he has almost achieved the position for which he is suited – undisputed leader of a party of one.

From the security of the buffalo's shoulders he could look down his beak at his former flock. He watched Laila Harre change her plumage. She discarded her parliamentary dress, reached into the back of her wardrobe and pulled out the leather bomber jacket. It's the plumage in which she feels comfortable. Thus bedecked she led her party off on migration to the place where they feel comfortable – the wilderness.

Predictable as a cuckoo clock, up popped the gnome of Tauranga, refreshed by a three-year sleep. He took down his dog-eared copy of the *Beginners' Book of Populist Rhetoric* and turned to page one. Can we fool them, he read. Yes we can, he thought and read no further.

All crows' feet and twinkle, he resembled a gentleman companion on a luxury liner. On went the charm and off went the old ladies. Their knees went feeble, juices flooded back into withered loins and the crones voted for the tango of hope.

The Greens danced to a different tune, but they danced too early. With a fortnight still to go they'd erected the maypole and were making whoopee. But then the music stopped and the country saw them as cranks once again. The whoopee went quiet and the maypole flopped.

But the sad story belongs to Mr English. Speights ads get it right. Bill got it wrong. He tried to be Southern man with northern grooming, and he plunged into Cook Strait with a stomach-churning splash. The polls plunged with him. The more he waved his arms and shouted 'Look at me', the lower he sank in the water. The more he asserted his conviction the less convincing he became.

'I believe,' said Bill but the other parties had stolen all the things he believed in. 'I believe I can convince you by making chopping movements with my hands. I believe that if I keep smiling you'll believe I'm happy. I believe that if I throw emphasis onto all *the* wrong words the more likely you are *to* give me your vote.' As his numbers fell he seemed to grow younger. By the end he looked like a schoolboy debater who'd lost his speech notes.

Only Mrs English believed. On the final night of failure when Bill came to the microphone in Gore with a mouthful of humble pie, Mrs English stared at her husband like a labrador expecting a walk.

And when the television interviewer got to him to twist the knife one last time, there was Mrs English still beaming over his shoulder. 'Behind you,' said Mike Hosking, 'your most loyal supporter.' Puzzled, Bill looked over his wrong shoulder. There was nobody there. He turned back to the camera looking like a lost little boy. It was excruciating, exquisite and exact.

Jules

Joseph Bennett, you stand before me . . .

Julian, m'lud. My Christian name's not Joseph. It's Julian.

But . . .

I know, m'lud. Both my friends call me Joe, but it's not my given name. I adopted it as a teenager.

Is that so?

It is, m'lud. Adolescence is a tough time, as I am sure m'lud will recall if he tosses his mind back a century or so. And it is made even tougher by being called Julian. At school, m'lud, they called me Jules. I yearned to be hard, m'lud. It is hard to be hard when one is called Jules. No one expects a Jules to be able to make a tackle on the rugby field.

And could you make a tackle?

No, m'lud. That was the problem. I had something wrong with my back.

You're not going to make that joke about there being a big yellow streak down it.

Not now, m'lud, no. But I was a cowardly rugby player.

So the perceived effeminate connotations of your given name drove you to change that name to the seemingly tougher Joe, even though the effeminate connotations were, in truth, bang on. In short, you were and you remain a slack-wristed non-tackling nancy boy.

Precisely, m'lud.

I can't say you surprise me. Anyway, Julian Bennett, you stand before me today charged with mockery of politicians and a refusal to treat seriously the business of the recent electoral campaign.

How do you plead?

Guilty, m'lud.

What? Come, come. Show some spine, for once. Put up your legal dukes.

I plead guilty to the charge, m'lud.

And to the additional charges of superficiality, levity, trivialisation and taking cheap shots?

Absolutely, m'lud, guilty as charged.

What, none of the customary liberal claptrap about freedom of speech, et bloody cetera?

None of that, m'lud.

So you're happy to be sentenced for reducing political debate to the level of a circus sideshow, for displaying, indeed, as little attention to serious and complicated matters of policy as the politicians did during the campaign?

I am, m'lud.

On the grounds, I presume, that you consider it apt and fitting to describe a superficial and clownish political performance in superficial and clownish terms.

Your words, m'lud.

Don't grovel, Jules.

Sorry, m'lud.

And so you imply that all elections, whether held in the agora of ancient Athens or in 100 per cent pure New Zealand, are essentially mood-driven and irrational popularity contests, and that both politicians and electorate expect it to be that way whatever they may say to the contrary?

I imply nothing, m'lud. You infer it.

Don't get clever, Jules. Are you also suggesting that the hard-won privilege of democracy, of power to the people, one person one vote, the peaceful submission to the will of the majority, is a notion so grand that we don't live up to it? That most people vote in a particular way because they have always voted that way, or because they feel some emotional warmth towards a candidate, or because they think there may be something in it for them?

I am suggesting nothing, m'lud. I have pleaded guilty.

Your guilt is for me to judge. Are you furthermore suggesting that because those in pursuit of power pander to that superficiality with their slogans and their airbrushed photographs, and that because they hire what I believe are called 'public relations consultants' in order to present themselves as bait to the fishy masses, you are justified in attacking them on precisely those superficial terms?

You said it, m'lud, not I.

And I suppose that underneath your petty bolshevism lurks the shop-worn belief that those who seek power are unlikely to be the people who should have it, and that the corrupting nature of power is as true today as it ever was, as illustrated by the current prime minister increasingly referring to herself in the third person, as 'The Prime Minister'.

I have pleaded guilty, m'lud.

And you're not going to try and weasel out of it with some trite nonsense about there being more truth in an ounce of comedy than in a hundredweight of seriousness?

I am not, m'lud. I am a convert to the metric system.

Enough. I have tired of you. I sentence you to publicise the name on your birth certificate. And may the Lord have mercy on your soul.

Dreams on wheels

My mother drives a hatchback. It's the sort of car in which you have to press the throttle to find out if the engine's running.

Two months ago my mother was taking me for a drive when a sports car overtook us. It was a sixties MG, all bucket seats and adolescence revisited. Like all sports cars it was designed to appeal to men too old to play sport.

As the MG passed, my mother sighed. 'Oh,' she said, 'I'd just love one of those.' My mother is seventy-nine. Naturally I was appalled.

I had thought my mother immune to whim. She belongs to a generation that did not indulge itself. Women like her wore printed cotton frocks and devoted their lives to rearing large families on carbohydrates and a single income.

To learn that even my mother could lust in secret for a car, underlined a truth of affluent society. Every vehicle is a wheeled aspiration. Every vehicle reflects its owner.

Most young men want a motor bike. A motor bike equates to freedom. It is the horsepower that snaps the apron strings, the oyster-knife that shucks open the world. It is wind in the hair and a throb between the legs. Whether or not a young man gets a motor bike depends on how much his parents dislike him.

My own motor bike was a moped. It went up hill quite well if you pedalled it. I loved that bike. I used to sing on it. I sang songs rich with adolescent grief or adolescent rapture. I bellowed my new-found manhood to the overarching sky. Once I swallowed a wasp. It made me crash. I had no excuse for my other crashes.

There are three ways to stop riding motor bikes. One is to do yourself damage. Another is to grow up. The third is to yield your motor bike to the police. I took the third option. As a result I missed the next phase of motorised life – the young person's car.

Young people drive heaps or phalluses. The heap is cheap, is poverty on wheels. It has rust, and vinyl, and keyless entry through the rear passenger window. You can sleep in a heap, or have sex in it, or tell lies about having sex in it. The heap is yesterday's car for tomorrow's people.

The phallus is tomorrow's car for today's hooligans. It's an enclosed motor bike. Based on designs for Apollo XVI its bonnet is longer than its passenger cell. It has fat tyres, gulping air intakes, a boombox, a fiercely farting exhaust and a spoiler at the back. The spoiler is named after the parents who paid for the car.

But the bike, the heap and the phallus are just rungs on the ladder towards middle age. Middle age is compromise and so is its car. That car is a saloon. It's the motorised equivalent of clothes from Farmer's. Though manufacturers take pains to promote the differences between saloons, the whole point of them is their similarity. Practical, sensible and dull as a suburb, saloons refuse to poke their heads above the parapet of conformity.

But there are alternatives. Those who have encumbered themselves with a vast brood forsake even the aerodynamic hints of a saloon. They acquire a people-carrier. It's a nine-seater semi-bus. It battles through the wind towards the future. The people-carrier announces to the world that the owner has surrendered all claim to independent personal life.

More assertive is the four-wheel drive all-terrain recreational vehicle. Rectilinear and butch, it resembles a shipping container on stilts. The owner still wants to compete. On the front a monstrous pair of bullbars to scatter rampaging herds of supermarket trolleys.

Beyond the all-terrain butchness comes the executive smoothness. Smug as a bank account, sleek as a suit, it glides from home to office, climate-controlled, equipped with everything, a motorised

Switzerland, self-contained, neutral, unassailable, purring with pleasure at itself.

But all is vanity and in the end the king of the road is time. Time makes people old and as they grow old they shrink. Their cars shrink with them. They shrink to those strange elevated narrow cars. They shrink to hatchbacks.

So when my mother said she yearned for a sports car, I gawped. I had never dreamed that she dreamed. But magnanimity is everything. 'Mother dear,' I said, 'old age should do as old age wishes. Mortgage the house, squander my inheritance, scour the country for a pink MG and scandalise the neighbours. Set the net curtains twitching and the tongues aclack. You are only old once. Follow your dreams. Buy that car.'

My mother looked at me. 'But I couldn't get in or out of it,' she said. So all, in the end, was well.

All squared away

It's all over. The final whistle's blown. I've lost, they've won and that's that. I've bought an iron.

Who 'they' are is hard to define. Call them the forces of conformity if you like but I think there's more to them than that. The forces come from within as much as without. My mind's been fingering the notion of an iron for several months. And just as when a customer fingers an item in a store, drifts elsewhere, then sidles back to finger it once more, and the alert shopkeeper knows that the thing is effectively sold, well, so it has proved with my iron. I am forty-five years old. My laundry cycle is finally complete.

Once upon a time in the lala land of infancy I had the knack of laundry. I gave it to my mother. She took it rumpled and soiled and gave it back smooth and smelling of air. But when I left home I forgot to take her with me. I also forgot to thank her. For I don't know how many handkerchiefs ironed square. For limitless pairs of cricket trousers with creases down the front, the grass stains on the knee scrubbed with a nail brush to faint brown ghosts of themselves.

For the next decade or so laundry bedevilled me. I delayed the doing of it. I would rescue T-shirts from the floor, sniff at their armpits and if my nose didn't wrinkle like a boxer dog's I'd steal another day. But eventually every T-shirt would be soiled to unwearability, every underpant to unspeakability and into a great black bin liner went the lot, into my pocket went a stash of change, and I would trudge all hunched and burdened to the laundrette.

Laundrettes the world over were identical. Crouched in some shaded part of town they never bothered to promote themselves with neon signs or advertising because the owner knew that if you didn't need to come you never would, but if you did, however horrible it was, you had no choice.

The streets they occupied were thick with litter and feral children and bitter urban misery. The single room was asthmatic with steam, as if the Amazon had been top-dressed with detergent. The machines were built industrially strong to stand the attentions of the poor of spirit. Above them notices explained in the simplest terms the modes of operation. You never read the notices. All machines worked the same. They had a little push-in tray with slots for coins. You emptied out your bin liner, holding your breath against the sudden pot-pourri of stale human emanations, then went outside to smoke and walk the desperate suburbs of the city for half an hour.

There were always enough washers. There were never enough driers. With your wet pile you stationed yourself in front of the drier with the least time to run on its dial. If the laundrette was empty the urge to cheat was fierce, to haul the unknown other's washing from the drier half done. The truly bold and cunning stopped two driers at once, emptied the first, transferred the washing from the second to the first, then placed his own in the second. I never dared.

I simply waited. It was longer than hospital waiting. When finally the drier fell to silence and either the proprietor claimed his washing or I, with slight distaste, unloaded the clothes, edgy with static, dumped them all unfolded in a pile – acceptable within the etiquette of laundrettes – and replaced them with my own I knew with slight relief that I was nearing bliss. The bliss of clean clothes. The bliss of a fortnight of freedom, a fortnight that would trickle by and as it trickled so the weight of dread would build, the knowledge that I'd soon once more have to revisit the stews of despair.

But then at thirty I tossed out my bin liner, stopped collecting change and bought a house. It came with a second-hand washing machine. I've got it still. I bless it.

But I never got an iron. If sometimes people pointed out the crumples in my shirts I said I didn't iron because my body wasn't square. I lied. I didn't iron because I didn't know how. And I didn't learn how because I was lazy. But, most significantly of all, I didn't iron because I didn't feel the need.

Why then should I now have fallen? Why in middle age should I spend time beside my jauntily striped Briscoes ironing board, squirting jets of steam on shirts and flattening the cloth? Is it just the gradual erosion into middle-class conformity? Perhaps it is. I never was a rebel. But I think there's something more to it than that. I think it may just be that I have bought an iron because I've noticed that my skin's begun to crease.

Giggle and bleed

What? 'Oh that, that's nothing. Nice of you to ask, but it's just a graze. Be gone in a week.

'Well, okay, rather a lot of grazes, but they're superficial. Healing nicely too. Wonderful, isn't it, the way the body rallies round – all those antiwhatsitsnames scurrying to the task like so many Florence Nightingales. Reassuring somehow.

'No, just on the wrists. Well, and elbows, of course, and a few on the chest, but really nothing to worry about. I mean, they won't leave scars or anything. Pity really. I rather cherish my scars. Testimony to a lived life, don't you think? See this one on my foot? Twenty-five years old that is. Got it at university from one of those ornamental wrought-iron gates with spikes. Up on the top of it I was and leaning backwards to give this sizeable lass a hand up, when suddenly there I was falling to earth and impaling myself on an upturned spike. Right through the foot. Me dangling upside down on this gate, giggling and bleeding, like a carcase on a butcher's hook.

'Yes, giggling.

'Oh I see, well, no, I suppose carcases don't giggle. But don't you think *Giggling and Bleeding* would make a rather good title for an autobiography?

'Okay, whatever. Anyway, next day the foot blew up like a melon. Lanced it myself. Pus came out like a tracer bullet. Shattered a light bulb. Ah youth. Great fun.

'No, I'm not avoiding the issue. There's nothing to tell.

'Well, if you really must know, in the gym.

'Yes, the gym.

'No, "gym bunny" is not the term I use. I just happen to think of my body as, if not a temple, at least a machine that deserves a bit of routine maintenance, so I toddle down the gym occasionally to give it an oil and lube, as it were, and no I'm not ashamed of that. Why should I be?

'Okay, perhaps most people don't get injured at the gym, but that doesn't mean there's an exciting story I'm keeping from you. As I seem to have said before, they're just grazes. Unlike this here where I fell down some French road works in the early eighties. Gravel got embedded in the flesh and two days later . . .

'Yes, as it happens, it *was* late at night. Why do you ask?

'No, I wasn't. In fact I rather resent the implication. I just tripped, that's all. And as I was saying, two days later I went to this French doctor who clearly hated me on sight and he sprinkled rubbing alcohol all over the wound and then attacked it with what I can only describe as a pot scourer. "This might sting a bit," he said. Sting! They had to peel me off the ceiling.

'You don't give up, do you? All right. Here's the story in full. I went to the gym and I fell off the treadmill. That's it. Happy now? Satisfied? On the treadmill one minute, off it the next. End of story.

'That's right, a sort of stationary running machine. But it was Mike's fault.

'Yes, Mike. He was standing behind me while I was running and I had to chat to him over my shoulder, which is a bit awkward when you're padding along at 12 kph. So I turned round.

'No, to be honest I was thinking about something else and I just presumed I could face the other way and keep running on the spot.

'Well actually Mike took most of the impact.

'Yes, I suppose so, mathematically – 24 kph. But you've got to laugh. I mean Mike and I just roared.

'Yes, after we'd picked ourselves up, that is. But if you can't laugh at yourself . . .

'Oh no, quite uninjured. Just shaken up a bit. The grazes came later. When I tried to get back on.

'Well, I don't know if you've ever tried to jump from a standing start onto a conveyor belt doing 12 kph. Somehow I ended belly down on the thing and just sort of lay there, feet wedged against the machine behind and with the belt grinding away underneath me.

'No, of course I didn't feel a fool. Could have happened to anyone. Indeed, I stayed there for several seconds smiling up at Mike and all the other people watching just to show it didn't hurt much.

'No, Mike turned the machine off.

'No, hardly bled at all. Just a bit of grazing. Unlike when I got this scar on my knee. What a beauty, eh? In Spain it was, about two in the morning. And what I'd still like to know is what the goat was doing there.'

Lovers by pen and gum

Dear Aunt Agony, I have two lovers. One is an MP, the other the head of a giant corporation. Both have written to me and showered me with gifts. What should I do? Yours, Torn

Dear Torn, Count your blessings. AA

Dear Aunt Agony, I'm not that sort of person. I believe in one lifelong soul-mate. Now I seem to have two of them and I feel, in the words of the immortal Sir Elton, like a candle in the wind. You are my last resort. Yours desperately, Still Torn

Dear Still Torn, Describe the gifts. AA

Dear Aunt Agony, A pen and a packet of chewing gum. Am at my wits' end. Please reply soonest. Yours wretchedly, Ripped to Shreds

Dear Ripped, Go for the richer one. Probably the pen. AA

Dear Aunt Agony, I'm not sure the pen is the richer one. He is the MP, a candidate in the coming election. He is called Right Honourable and those words do something funny to my tummy. Around the time of the last election we had a brief fling. He wrote to ask if I had anything on my mind. I wrote back saying yes, him. Since that time almost three years of silence. I'd begun to think he might be frightened of commitment.

But today the pen arrived. It is a beautiful blue and white plastic ballpoint with his name on the barrel. From time to time I clutch it to my . . . well anyway, let's just say I clutch it. The pen came with a card inviting me to write back. All day I have tried to find the words to say all that I feel about him in the six lines available on the card. When I finally settled on what to write, the pen wouldn't work. Had I been clutching it for too long? Or is he trying to tell me something? Yours, On the Horns of a Dilemma

Dear On the Horns, Go for the chewing gum. AA

Dear Aunt Agony, Do you really think so? His name is Mr Wrigley and he's very forward. The chewing gum he sent is called X-cite. If that isn't suggestive I don't know what is. But it came with a beautifully written letter. 'X-cite,' writes Mr Wrigley, 'is more than a mint and more than a gum. X-cite combines both in a totally unique way.' That's how I have always imagined a relationship – something not just unique but totally unique. 'Take on the shattering crunch,' continues Mr Wrigley, 'or linger over the flavour sensation. Enjoy, share, reload.' I have done all these things except share. Some things are too private to share. I feel, in the immortal words of Sir Paul, that all you need is love. Do you agree?

On the side of the packet of chewing gum there's a little red tab. 'You control the X-cite experience,' says Mr Wrigley. 'The countdown starts when you pull the red tab.' Except when I pulled the red tab the only thing that happened was some chewing gum fell out. Did I do something wrong? Or is Mr Wrigley trying to tell me something?

What do you advise? Yours, Split down the Middle

Dear Split, The singles bar. There's a nice one in Durham Street. AA

Dear Aunt Agony, I don't think you understand. I have spent my life waiting for the L word, and now I am overwhelmed. Whenever I think of the MP, I feel, in the immortal words of Sir Mick, like jumping Jack Flash. But then I think of Mr Wrigley and my heart, in the immortal words of Sir Cliff – or was it Lady Lulu? – goes boom bang a bang. You're the only person I can turn to. Yours, In Torment

Dear In, Has it ever crossed that pound and a half of greyish-pink bubble wrap that you are pleased to call your mind that your little lover boys think no more of you than they do of ethics; that what they write is parody; that one offers the parody of taking an interest in you, while the other offers the parody of a thrill; that their words are Trojan; that they are trying to sneak into the sleeping fortress of your head under the guise of something other than what they are; that to the MP you are a voter, and to Mr Wrigley you are that most gruesome of things, a consumer; that the one wants a tick in the box and the other a dollar in the till; and that you would be well advised, in the words of the immortal but inexplicably undubbed William Shakespeare, to daub the walls of a jakes with them? Yours sincerely, AA

Dear Aunt Agony, What's a jakes? Yours, Puzzled.

At two drunks swimming

As any safety enthusiast will tell you, drinking and swimming don't mix. And as any drunk will tell the safety enthusiast, nuts.

The safety wallah will say that out of every thousand drunks who go swimming, one drowns. The drunk will say that he's never seen a thousand drunks swimming.

Anyway, there were only two of us, so it was a statistical near-certainty that the drunk who drowns was still in the pub. Well, actually, there were four of us, if you include the dogs, and we did.

The trip to the bay was the barman's idea. My other excuses are that I was drunk, that my dog likes swimming, that I like swimming with her, that it had been a hot day, and that it was midnight.

The problem with a hot day is that it doesn't happen at midnight. A southerly had risen. The waves were a couple of feet tall and fringed with cream. But we were committed, and the dogs were exultant.

The barman stood on the rail of the jetty in his trendy swimming togs. I stood on the bottom step of the jetty in my sky-blue Warehouse underpants. The barman finished his cigarette, tossed it into the sea in a glowing arc and followed it. I finished my cigarette, tossed it into the sea in a glowing arc and stayed where I was.

The coolest man I ever saw was standing on the high board above a French swimming pool, smoking. He had the body of a decathlete. People were looking up at him. He knew they were looking up at him. When he neared the end of his cigarette he wrapped his tongue round the filter, withdrew it into his mouth and dived. Then he surfaced, rolled onto his back, unfurled his tongue and carried on smoking.

From the water the barman called his dog. The dog is young, loyal and stupid. While I stood admiring the goosebumps on my arms, it bounded past me and launched itself. Dogs dive badly. They start paddling before they hit the water. And they land on their bellies.

The smack when the dog hit the water made me wince. The dog did not wince. It was away, black and happy in the black water.

I was not away. I called to the swimming barman to count down from three. On three, I crouched. On two, I breathed in. On one, I swung my arms back. On go, I stood up again. The barman said something provocative. I dived. The water was surprisingly warm. My sky-blue Warehouse underpants came off.

My dog appeared beside me, her legs frantic under the water. She snorts as she swims, but she can swim for miles. I can't.

All females float. Nine out of ten white males float. I am the tenth. If I lie still in water I sink. Apparently most black men sink too. I suppose that is why you see few black swimmers in the Olympics.

At the same time, you see lots of black runners. The conclusion to draw, I suppose, is that if you're a white man being chased by a black man, you should head for water. If you're a black man being chased by a white man, run. And if you've got one white parent and one black parent, you should be fine.

I didn't suppose all this at the time. I was trying to swim towards a raft anchored in the middle of the bay. It went in and out of view with the waves. I got mouthfuls of salt.

I lost my dog behind a wave and I worried about her. Then I felt a twinge of cramp in my calf and I worried about me. The raft seemed a long way away.

I hate seaweed. When it slithers against my chest it reminds me of the depths of black water below. I do not like to be so reminded. I can think of few deaths worse than drowning. People say that your life passes in front of your eyes. Perhaps it does, but with water in my airways I doubt if I'd sit back with popcorn to watch it. Anyway, I've seen it before.

People also say drowning is peaceful. I don't know how they know. And of all the opposites of peaceful, one of the most emphatic is having water in your airways.

I veered towards the shore. I couldn't see my dog, or the barman's dog, or the barman, or any pleasure in what I was doing. I wanted solidity under me. I was fighting the water and panic.

I heard barking and saw my dog on the path above me. That made the last ten yards easy. I hauled myself onto the rocks like something primeval evolving. My dog fussed about me. I picked my way along the gravel path towards my clothes, naked, teeth chattering like a typewriter, acutely aware of being Lear's 'poor bare forked animal'.

The barman had swum to the raft and back.

'Great, wasn't it,' he said.

I said I'd been scared.

'Yeah,' he said, 'great, isn't it.' And I had to admit that it was. Afterwards. Scared is good, afterwards.

Dawn ducks

Ducks swim with serenity, but they walk like comics. Their feet are set too far back on their bodies. They lurch across land, like children learning to march who swing the right leg and the right arm forward at the same time.

I am driving to the airport at dawn. Steinbeck called dawn 'the hour of the pearl', a secret time when 'cats drip over fences'. I see no cats. And in the ghost light, at first I see only one duck. It is standing in the east-bound lane of Brougham Street beside something shapeless. As I drive closer I see that the something is a splatter of blood and organs and feathers. A tuft of blue-tipped wing feathers shows it was a drake. Do ducks mate for life? I don't know. It is Sunday. There is almost no traffic.

To be up early on a Sunday is to feel outside the mainstream, to belong to a club of outsiders. The world is sleeping, catching the rest denied by the workaday week. The few people about are those whose jobs never stop – nurses coming off duty, telephone operators, deliverers of bread, night-shift factory hands, security guards. And among them perhaps a few party-goers who have woken dry, cramped and bleary on a sofa amid bottles and felt the sudden need for home.

The Sunday quiet won't last. It died with God. The old traffic-free, stiff-collared, bored-child, Sunday-best Sundays now exist only in sepia. The modern Sunday throbs with trade. The congregations drive to the malls.

I have a plane to catch and I drive past the duck on the other side of the road. A green van is going the other way. In my mirror I watch the duck waddle a few steps towards the verge and the van swerve slightly to be sure of missing it. Then the duck returns to its vigil beside the corpse. It stands and waits, as baffled as five thousand generations of philosophers by the abrupt and incontrovertible punctuation of death. No sign of distress. No thought of litigation. No self-pity. It just waits.

Poets have done death. They've also done dawn. 'Earth has not anything to show more fair,' wrote Wordsworth on London Bridge as the sun came up two hundred years ago and it irks me a little that I cannot help seeing the morning through the lens of his words.

The airport forecourt still has that sleep-rubbed-from-the-eyes feel. An engine like a golf buggy sweeps dog-ends from the gutter and into its sucking belly. Taxi-drivers wait inside their sleek white vehicles, newspapers spread across steering wheels. Courier vans draw up, and the drivers run with boxes through automatic plate glass doors.

Inside, the airport is air-conditioned and awake. Security checks. A flock of Asian tourists with impeccably ironed clothes and far too much luggage. The steam-engine noises of a coffee machine.

The stewardesses welcome me aboard with dental-advertisement smiles. I am assured that my safety is their priority. I ignore the pantomime of oxygen masks and whistles on life-jackets, and the video screen that lowers eerily to show a box-office hit called 'Important Health and Safety Information'.

As we rise from the ground the sun is rising out of Pegasus Bay, stretching a gold road across the satin-smooth water with the rumpled edge. And up pops Browning.

Round the Cape of a sudden came the sea
And the sun looked over the mountain's rim;
And straight was a path of gold for him,
And the need of a world of men for me.

The world of men, of business, is taking me north for the day. Over the lower North Island a thick fleece of cloud. The sun gilds its ridges. The cloud looks as though if you jumped into it you would bounce, slowly. Up through the middle of it poke two volcanoes. The stewardess brings me an omelette in a box and it tastes just as I imagine the clouds would taste.

The cloud has a sharply defined edge like a television weather map. Beyond it I can see the long gleam of Hawke Bay.

By the time we land in Auckland the day is fully under way. I go about my mundane business, talking to people, laughing, drinking befuddling lunchtime wine. I fly back in the late afternoon. By the time I am driving again on Brougham Street the light has thickened. There is a single dark smudge on the road, no feathers, and no sign of the other duck. And a Sam Hunt poem about a possum surfaces in my head.

For our convenience

Dr Killjoy and Sister Grumbles are at it again. They want all the dogs of Christchurch to be tethered to their owners when in public.

Of course my first reaction was disbelief. Could they be serious that no dogs should run free? I read the piece again. They could. They were. And the Christchurch City Council, bless their pretty little chains of office, has listened to them.

Disbelief gave way to outrage and with outrage came malediction. I cursed Dr Killjoy. I cursed Sister Grumbles. I cursed them high and I cursed them wide. May their Dowson's footwear, I cursed, land unerringly in poop. May they subscribe to Sky. May their houses get termites and their children worms. May their soft furnishings fade and their oven doors explode and may they watch *Fair Go* until their brains turn to soup. May they have invested in Enron.

I resolved to flee. I would tuck my dog in one pocket and a sandwich in the other and we would head for saner pastures, for the wide beaches of freedom in the country of Elsewhere.

But even as I planned my flight, my spine stiffened. Because here at last was a cause. I have never had a cause. The greats of yesterday stole all the causes. Those greats were scourged or flayed or toasted for their causes but they died with grins as wide as letterboxes. For they knew that they'd find immortality in the display case of history.

Now I would join them. On the day the by-law was enacted I would stride into the council chamber and let slip the dog of war. Her name is Jessie. And as she bounded towards the mayoral throne in the hope of a pat I would stand strong against the agents of tyranny. Let the jacks-in-office flip the tops of their flip-top notebooks. Let them lick their pencils. Let them record the details of my crime. They would only be carving my name in granite and gold. Their dinky uniforms and hats would bed down to compost before my name would fade. Defensor Canis, I would be, a virtuous outlaw, a Robin Hood, a man whose spine would not buckle under injustice.

But then above the swelling bass-note of rebellion I heard a different note. It was the piping treble of pity. Pity for Dr Killjoy. Pity for Sister Grumbles. Because the Zeitgeist has poisoned their souls. Theirs is the way of the world to come. A sour, thin way, the future's dismal cul-de-sac.

For this proposal goes far beyond dogs. It springs from two emotions that are increasingly influential. One is arrogance. The other is fear. Both are base.

Have the doc and his bloodless woman no sense of a dog's need to run? They have not. Do they not care that their proposal would be cruel? They do not. Because in their arrogance they believe that only the human species has any right to draw joy from the world.

When dogs exult in freedom in the park, when dogs play games for the fun that is in them, when dogs cavort in the present tense, they grant a glimpse of something we've lost. They simply revel in being alive. They don't fret for their share portfolios. They don't hunch over pornography. They run with the wind and they pant with zest. It does my dog good to run. It does me good to run with her. Dr K and Sister G would excise that good.

They want to take us all one step further down the path to a sanitised world. A shopping-mall world. A world of endless consumption of tat until we peg out. A world as sterile as a hospital ward. A horrid pointless bloodless colourless world, a world ruled by Starbucks and the six o'clock news and OSH. A world of plastics and disc jockeys and car grooming.

Why should they want this? Because they are afraid.

Children get it right. Last week I took my dog to a primary

school. Two hundred children rushed to stroke her. She took it on the chin. And on the ears and the tail and the neck.

But if Dr K and Sister G win the day the children will be taught to fear. They will learn that my dog is dirty, and that the planet owes them a living. They will be taught that society is hostile, and then they will be surprised when it becomes hostile. They will be disabled by fear. Their blood will be watered to transparency. And we shall have arrived at the future. It will look like Disneyland. Disneyland where people are fat and the thrills synthetic. Disneyland where the lawns are rectilinear and death is banned. Disneyland where the only animals are stuffed monstrosities with floppy ears and imbecilic grins, apart of course from those animals whose tongues and guts and nostrils have been ground into hamburger patties and smeared with mustard the colour of pus. For our convenience.

Not quite death in the afternoon

Igave up rugby in 1997. The decisive moment arrived when I realised not only that I didn't want to tackle anyone but also that I didn't want the ball. I left the field in a blaze of self-awareness. And if I'd auctioned my boots right then I would now be able to move my shoulder.

The damage was done last Friday in Lyttelton Supervalue. One moment I was sunk in gastronomic reverie amid the tins of haricots au jus de tomates and pain blanc au sac plastique, the next I was backed up against a refrigerated display of certified genuine olde Englishe sausages and being subjected to a stream of flattery so transparent that I took a few pieces home to repair the greenhouse.

The upshot of this encounter was that on Saturday afternoon I found myself on a suburban park in an autumnal breeze and my ancient rugby boots. The opposition stood in the distance quietly grazing. They comprised seven big men and eight huge men, bedecked in fetching blue jerseys that matched my funk.

My teeth were shrouded in a plastic mouthguard that had lain untouched for six years and for the contents of which I had turned down several substantial bids from an eminent mycologist.

I was there partly out of pity. My interlocutor in the supermarket had spiked the long drink of flattery with a sharp cry of woe. 'We need you, Joe,' he said, 'not just because you're the most talented ex-loose forward to enter this aisle of the supermarket in the last thirty seconds, but also because we're short.'

He wasn't wrong. None of my comrades in arms stood more than 5 foot 10, which in metric terms is two furlongs shy of a line-out jumper. But what they lacked in height they made up for in age. Indeed I recognised most of them from my retirement function when they tearfully farewelled me from the club with the traditional salute of two raised fingers. Even the grizzled old captain was there, still suffering from the rare medical condition that renders him unable to run without shouting. In the waistband of his shorts a pension book flapped.

But there were also a few younger things, several of whom were sons of team mates, children whose rattles I had tossed back into the pram. And the number eight was a youth who had shown such promise that he had once been entrusted into my care in that breeding ground of stars, the Christ's College Under 14 Cs.

A substantial crowd had gathered, reminiscent of the mob who used to roll up for those bottom-of-the-table clashes featuring the Colosseum Christians.

As every top sportsman will tell you, there is a moment just before the start of a contest when the senses are tuned to an altogether higher pitch. Thus I was able to detect at one and the same time the fragrant drip of my armpits, the ruminant belches of the opposition, and the wail of a circling ambulance.

The game began well with the ball being kicked to the far side of the field. Timing my jog to perfection I arrived in time to assist several of my team mates to their feet, reset their limbs and point them in the direction of a tackle that urgently needed making.

Trotting around the park at a discreet distance from the ball proved a tolerable way of spending the afternoon, until I sought a moment or two of repose on top of a comfortable-looking ruck. There I met a forearm whose progress I chose to impede with the bridge of my nose.

The blood bin consisted of a patch of mud and a moustached Florence Nightingale, who urged me to shove a wodge of vaseline up each nostril and get back out there. Dizzied I may have been by the sight of my own blood, a fluid of which I am fond but whose existence I am happy in civilian life to take on trust, but I am prepared to swear that he added the word 'nancy'.

Stung by the slur, I returned to the field with such reckless impetuosity that I found myself stationed between the try line and a ball-carrying opponent. The gentleman in question had had his neck surgically removed in order to allow him to pass through doorways with only a little stooping. The surgeon had also taken the opportunity to sew a hogshead into the man's stomach.

Pausing only to ring my lawyer about an ambiguous codicil, I drove my shoulder into the hogshead. When I sat up several yards from the point of impact it was to the sight of Goliath celebrating. 'Great try,' I said. He looked at me. 'Sir,' I added.

The rest of the game passed in a blur of self-preservation that was not entirely successful. At the final whistle the damage inventory consisted of a road kill nose, a finger like an olde Englishe sausage and a shoulder whose rotator cuff will rotate barely sufficiently to lift a gavel. But lift a gavel it will.

What am I bid for one pair of boots?

Girlie sox

Are you a sturdy independent, one who stands strong and rooted when the winds of fashion blow, one who disdains the mob, who proclaims 'no coward soul is mine', who stands for what he stands for and who rises above fad? Me too. And yet I've bought three pairs of girlie socks.

Girlie socks are the socks you wear when you pretend not to be wearing socks. Professional female tennis players have always worn girlie socks. And although professional female tennis players grow more muscular every year, and although they grunt like mastodons – or at least how I imagine mastodons would have grunted, which is effortfully – they still, the tennis players that is and not the mastodons, wear girlie socks. At their girliest these socks have a pink bobble on the back to stop the sock shrivelling into the shoe.

My girlie socks do not have a pink bobble on the back. Nevertheless I cannot deny their girliness. Nor can I pretend they are an error. I drove to the Warehouse, strode through home appliances and stationery and reached menswear after a mere fifteen minutes. I studied the sock racks. I fingered and I pondered. For as long as I have been buying my own socks the result of this exercise has never varied. I have come away from the store with emphatically non-girlie socks. But not any more.

I can understand why female tennis players wear girlie socks. By being hidden in the shoe, girlie socks make legs look longer. Longer legs are sexier legs. What is harder to understand is why I should now wear them. My legs are as long as they need to be. Though they satisfactorily link my buttocks to my feet, my legs do not excite me and forty-five years of experience suggest that I would be unwise to expect them to excite others. Nevertheless I have now encased the southern ends of those legs in long-leg-making girlie socks.

Since I was seventeen I have played squash in the sort of white ankle socks that used car salesmen in the eighties wore with slip-on shoes. I am pleased to report that the car salesmen have forsaken those socks, but I have persisted with them for squash. I have found them cheap and satisfactory.

They are made in some factory in Pakistan or Taiwan where the workers earn a dollar a day. I have never cared about these workers because I have never met them. If I did meet them I imagine that I would still not care.

I have worn a thousand pairs of their socks until the heel in each has withered from a cushion of fluff to a transparent but indestructible lattice of nylon. When a sock reaches that point I put it in a drawer. Five years later I come across it curled and grey like corpse skin, and I throw it away. But each sock has done its duty. Honest traditional ankle socks, convenient, cheap, serving their purpose, the dull foot soldiers in the hosiery war. But now I have forsaken them for girlie socks.

Money does not explain my change of heart. Girlie and non-girlie socks were the same price. Colour does not come into it either. White is white. A man with whom I used to play squash, now cruelly killed by cancer, used to play in unmatching fluorescent socks. But though I admired him and though he regularly beat me and laughed as he did so, I could never emulate him. I am a white sock man.

The only reason I can offer for my shift into girlie socks is, well, take down your photo album. Turn, if you are old enough, to the seventies. Stare at the flares and the hair and the chunky shoes and the cheesecloth shirt with the tear-drop collar. Or the hot-pants or the maxi-skirt or the, well, you get the picture. Indeed you've got the picture. For once the camera, source of a million lies, doesn't lie.

To put it with cruel simplicity, I bought my girlie socks because they are the fashion and other men have started wearing them. And though I have openly scoffed at those men, and though I have rightly observed that girlie socks offer no advantages over ankle socks, nevertheless, gradually, regrettably, but inevitably, I have come to see my ankle socks as staid, as ugly, as the sporting equivalent of the knee-length walk socks of the holidaying bureaucrat.

Have you ever seen a million starlings coming in to roost at dusk? They wheel like a living cloud, darkening the sky, forming one minute a spinning upward vortex, the next a diving arrowhead, driven by God knows what imperative and all of them squealing. Listen closely to that squeal. 'No coward soul is mine,' proclaims each starling. 'I am a sturdy independent.'

Cheap and stationary

Contentment is undervalued. The Zeitgeist sneers at contentment. My hopelessly old-fashioned dictionary defines contentment as the condition of being adequately happy, and in these exciting times that just won't do. Contentment lacks thrust. It lacks drive. It lacks ambition. What we're supposed to prefer is fun, novelty, thrills, all the stuff that gets packed in with that word of the moment, experience.

I've got a plan for experience. I'm going to beckon it round the back of the garage with a sugar cube and then I'm going to bop it on the head with a mallet. There will be intense joy in watching it shrivel and die.

No more wilderness experience, overseas experience, sightseeing experience, or, oh dear me, quality shopping experience, the lure of which is supposed to winch us off the sofa and down to the local mall where the Muzak and the air-conditioning and the windowloads of tat in primary colours sing the siren songs of consumption, urging us to plunge deep into the wallet and deeper into debt in pursuit of the eternally elusive. That's what the Zeitgeist orders. It's called growth. It's called prosperity. What it isn't called is contentment.

Contentment's cheap and stationary. It doesn't require a set of patio furniture, a three-ring barbecue with hood, or a wardrobeful of self-replicating shoddy from China. Nor does it require foreign travel, or a kayak and a boiling river, or a bungy rope or an aerodynamic motor car with gross superfluous power that can pin us to the back of the seat and make our faces white with fear. In particular contentment doesn't stimulate whatever gland it is that pumps out that overrated emergency chemical adrenalin. I would happily take the mallet to the thick-lensed chemist who discovered adrenalin. He gave the marketing pimps exactly what they wanted. They've sold it as the holy grail of being happy. But it doesn't grant contentment.

Contentment is watching a hen take a dust bath. The hen is okay. It's got a belly full of grain and as there's nothing else it needs to be doing right now it waddles wisely off to the thin dry soil under the gum tree. It scratches itself a hollow and snuggles there. It squirms its breast and belly into the dust, puffing its feathers to spread the dust through them. It scratches dust up over its back. It stretches each wing with the luxuriance of a dog stretching its spine. Then it just lies there dusted and content. If a hen could smile it would smile in a dust bath.

My own contentment is P.G. Wodehouse. Give me a sofa, a Wodehouse and an empty afternoon and I'm a hen in the dust. Wodehouse spent eighty-odd years knocking up stories. None of them bears the least reference to reality. And all of them are couched in a prose so elegant and funny and simple that I'd happily marry it. You emerge from a Wodehouse story with no new knowledge of the world, with a conviction that you have spent the afternoon to absolutely no practical purpose and therefore with a deep sense of contentment. In short you've done an Emsworth.

Lord Emsworth is not Wodehouse's most famous creation but he should be. He's a hero for our times. He loves his pig. The pig is called the Empress of Blandings and she has won numerous medals for fatness.

Emsworth's idea of a good day is to spend the morning leaning on the rails of the sty and admiring the Empress. Having looked his fill on the good pig, Emsworth likes to pass the afternoon dozing or sniffing roses. And in the evening he immerses himself in Whiffle on *The Care of the Pig*.

Emsworth feels about Whiffle as I feel about Wodehouse. 'Lord Emsworth turned back and with infinite relief discovered that he was alone. His niece had disappeared. He took up Whiffle on *The Care of the Pig* and had just started to savour once more the perfect prose of that chapter about swill and bran-mash, when the door opened.'

The door is always opening on Emsworth and when it opens trouble walks in. It walks in in the form of people who want to get things done, the foes of contentment, bullying aunts, fearsome sisters, love-lorn nieces and Baxter. Baxter is Lord Emsworth's secretary. He is known to Lord Emsworth as the efficient Baxter, and in Lord Emsworth's lexicon efficient is not a term of endearment. Baxter wants to do. Emsworth wants to be.

And it is Baxter who is in tune with the times we live in, Baxter who embraces the Zeitgeist. In the dynamic, exciting, prosperous, riven, thrill-seeking twenty-first century, the wisdom of Emsworth, the vacuous ninth earl, the high priest of the dust bath of contentment, has been lost.

His favourite word is and

I taught Hemingway's great-grandson. Or it may have been his great-nephew, I don't remember. Anyway it was in Canada some twenty years ago and the boy was called Hemingway and he was a nice kid.

I thought of him today because I've been reading Hemingway again. Sometimes I like Hemingway and other times I don't. He writes this macho simple style of prose that's full of veins and sinews like the back of a gravedigger's hand. Sometimes I believe it. Other times I don't. His favourite word is and. He doesn't go for fancy words like although.

His great-grandson or whatever didn't write simple macho prose that was full of veins and sinews, but as I say he was a nice kid. He laughed a lot. The school was an old-fashioned place and there was cricket. No one played cricket in that part of Canada except that school. Young Hemingway took a shine to cricket and wanted a cricket bat and I organised to get one for him. It had to be imported and it cost as much as I earned in a month, but the boy had a rich father with a helicopter and a motor boat so that was all right. The second time the kid used the bat it broke.

But anyway I am reading a collection of Hemingway's journalism. Some of it is good and some of it is tired. Beneath it all runs the voice of the man like a deep river. I still don't know whether I believe the sound of that river but it is tempting to believe it because the rhythm of the language is hypnotic. Hemingway writes about things simply and he seduces me.

He did a lot of shooting. He shot pheasant and curlew and teal and partridge and woodcock. He writes how geese look as if they are flying slow but really they fly fast and so the first goose any shooter kills is the one two behind the one he's aiming at. I don't want to shoot geese but I like that detail. I've shot one bird, a chaffinch. The bird fell straight down and I walked across and picked it up warm and stroked its million bright and tiny feathers and felt bad. Hemingway never felt bad about shooting things, or at least he never said he felt bad about shooting things. Nor do the men in his novels ever feel bad about shooting things. They are tough spare men with hands like gravediggers. They don't say much.

And on page 185 in this book I was reading this afternoon Hemingway tells the story of the first time he shot a quail. It was already dead. He found it and put a bullet through its corpse and then lied to his father that he shot it on the wing. In bed that night 'I remember crying with my head under the patchwork quilt after he was asleep because I had lied to him. If he would have waked up I would have told him.'

I read that last sentence and then I read it again. The sentence was grammatically wrong. The sequence of tenses was wrong. It was the sort of sentence that his great-grandson or nephew might have written when I was teaching him cricket and English. And I would have underlined the sentence in pencil and written in the margin what was wrong with it. It wouldn't have made any difference. Correcting essays never made any difference but you kept doing it because that's what English teachers do.

I guess that old man Hemingway got the sentence wrong on purpose. Perhaps he wanted to seem rough and simple. Perhaps he wanted to write as men speak. But no one writes as men speak and he must have known that. Write down the words men actually speak and you get a page of gibberish.

And now I don't know if it matters that the sentence is grammatically wrong. I understand the sentence fine. And I recognise the feeling. I once cheated in a cross-country race and I lied to my father about it and I knew he didn't believe me but I stuck to my story because I had to. That was thirty-five years ago and I remember it still and it's too late to take back the lie because my father's dead. And Hemingway's dead. And the Hemingway I

60

taught must now be about thirty-five and going bald and I expect he's got kids. And when I think of those things I think that getting grammar right doesn't matter as much as all that. And if I would have been a braver kid with gravedigger's hands I would have told my father I had lied to him. And if I would have been a better man I wouldn't have shot the chaffinch.

Go and eat sky

Ibought some words today. Here are nine of them. 'Please leave, honey. I cook an enormous black whisper.'

Overall there were about three hundred words and they cost me $45. Here are four more of them. 'Go and eat sky.'

Most were ordinary words like those, words I already knew, short words of good stout Anglo-Saxon pedigree, rather than their fancy sisters born of other linguistic families. There were no words like mammothrept. Instead there were words like these five: 'A gift of fiddle juice'.

I am not the first person to pay $45 for these words. Indeed, according to the pretentious leaflet that came with the words, I am about the three millionth.

The words are written on little magnets. You can fix the magnets to the chrome-finish cappuccino maker that you never use, or, since the magnets grip like limpets, to the bonnet of your car. Or I suppose you could even slip the words under your mattress and sleep on them to relieve the multiplicity of aches that time afflicts us with. But everyone I know who's bought these words has stuck them on the fridge, and there composed sentences like 'Club that egg, mother'.

The first word I picked out from my box of words was 'dream'. From my desk I tossed 'dream' at the fridge door five feet away, hoping that it would fix itself there with a tiny but satisfying slap. But 'dream' struck the fridge at an angle and fell to the floor. My dog sniffed at 'dream' and found it inedible. I tossed 'music'. 'Music' fell too.

My fridge is full of beer. The first word that stuck to the fridge door was 'never'. The second, and it landed smack alongside, was 'drunk'. And there you have the charm of these magnetic words. They throw up surprises and ironies. Surprises and ironies are good.

For words can get into ruts. And when they get into ruts they die. Instead of throwing light on the world, words in ruts have lost touch with it. They bespeak no fresh experience.

Rutted words are clichés. And, as Martin Amis observed, we should all be foot soldiers in the war against cliché. We should point the Uzi at 'learning curves' and 'worst-case scenarios'. We should point it at 'roller-coaster rides' and 'rocket science' and 'climate of opinion'. My own hatred of 'hard yards' is so intense that the next time I hear the phrase I shall personally hang and draw the speaker. And as he dangles from the gibbet with his gut split open, I shall use his large intestine to spell out in cursive script the injunction, 'Thou shalt think for thyself'. I shall use his short intestine to add 'dolt'. Quartering the victim thereafter will be a kindness.

Words have other dangers beyond becoming clichés. They can, for example, be used emotively as they are in the lyrics of popular music. It's all trash. It shuffles into a thousand banal variations a vocabulary that even the most feeble mammothrept would be ashamed of. And then a hundred identical radio stations pump the trash across the airwaves. It acts like a soporific. It turns the mind to pulp.

No doubt popular music also puzzles the extra-terrestrial eavesdroppers. They shake their several hundred heads and mutter that here must be an easy planet to conquer. Its dominant species seems to have forsaken consecutive thought. It has divorced language from meaning. It is proud to throw its arms and legs about while chanting that it lives in a yellow submarine.

And furthermore, words can lie. With words I can say black is white. I can say, 'Thank you very much for the aftershave.' I can say, 'Bang right, Mr Peters.'

My dog has no words and so she cannot lie. When Mr Peters knocks on my door she can only tell him the truth with her keen white teeth.

Words can stultify, words can deceive and words can kill. Words are not the world. They are no substitute for reality. The word 'knife' cannot stab you. We should show more respect to things than we do to words.

But, and here is the paradox that my magnetic words underline, words can make new. By shifting the three hundred words on the fridge I can arrive at combinations that make my head fizz. I can open a realm of possibility.

Words are our handles on the world. They are all that we have to think about it with. Used as they should be, they can peel the eyes and freshen the mind and bring delight. And they can even earn money.

For two nights ago in the Volcano a man asked me the strangest word I knew. I said it was a word that meant 'a spoilt child raised by its grandmother'. He said it was not a word one could use in a newspaper column. I said it was. Indeed I bet him I could use the word three times in a single column. The bet was $20. The word was mammothrept.

Put that head back

Damn him. He's a doom-sayer. He also happens to be a nice bloke but that makes no difference. Damn him, I say. He's done a Pandora on me.

By trade he's a mechanic. He keeps my car going. It's an old car that should long since have retired to the automotive rest home to grind its gums and watch daytime television. That it hasn't is testimony to the mechanic's skill, but still I say damn him.

My car drinks a little oil. It stutters a little on cold mornings. But it is a trusted ally and we have a sort of symbiosis. It knows my needs, I its. It knows I don't want to growl through the streets belching testosterone. And I know that my car doesn't want to leave the tarseal, that if I took it down the off-road tracks to where the best fishing is, it would rattle, wheeze and die. I am as fond of my car as it is possible for me to be of a machine. It serves.

Last week I went to fetch it after its six-monthly spruce-up at the garage. There I signed the usual amusing cheque for tappet realignment, sprocket sharpening, bleeding and road-testing the odometer, and all the other mysteries that act on the bill like a foot pump. But I paid, as I always do, without demur, and I nodded patiently at the mechanic's technical explanations in the way that a congregation attends a ritual conducted in Latin, believing that somehow, for all its impenetrability, the mumbo jumbo must be doing some good, acting as a shield against the unseen hovering nasties of the air. In short I paid my bill in the manner of a tribe offering a virgin to the witchdoctor.

But then the witchdoctor stepped beyond his brief. 'Have you,' he asked, 'had the cam belt done?'

What is a cam belt? How does one have it done? How can one tell a done cam belt from an undone one? I gawped. He explained. Apparently the cam belt should be done every 80,000 k. My car has travelled 265,000 k. At the same time – and here is the cruelty of the thing – to do my cam belt would cost more than the car is worth. So I am left driving a car whose cam belt could go at any time without warning.

And though what the mechanic told me was well meant, and though what he told me was true, and though what he told me was theoretically of use to me and right for him to say, I wish he'd said nothing.

There are several versions of the myth of Pandora's Box. They all involve Pandora and, astonishingly, a box. The box contained the evils of the world. Pandora's curiosity made her open it and out flew the evils to bedevil us for ever. But the version of the myth that makes most sense to me is that when Pandora saw what she had done she slammed the lid back down and caught the last of the evils amidships. Half of the final evil escaped and half did not. That evil was knowledge of the future.

The myth seems exact to me because we do half-know the future. The details are missing but we know in general terms how things will pan out. I know that a decade from now my car will be dead. I know that within four decades I'll have joined it at the wrecker's. But there is nothing to be gained from that knowledge.

For though fools still dabble with tea leaves, horoscopes and tarot cards, to know the future in all its detail would be an x-rated curse. It would paralyse us. Beside the text of one's life it would constantly be scribbling 'vanity' in the margin. So we behave as if we didn't know what we half-know. The whole charm of being alive is that the sun rises fresh tomorrow, that a page is turned and it appears to be both blank and pregnant with possibility.

But my mechanic put paid to a part of that. Now when I drive my car I am conscious of my cam belt. It can hear it perishing. I can sense its last strand stretching to the point of going ping. And when it pings I shall be left immobile.

All of which I can cope with when it happens. I have no mechanical skill but I will survive. What I find hard to cope with is the constant gnawing knowledge that it could be about to happen.

There are three tenses, past, present and future. To live in the past is sad. To have some sense of the future is prudent. But despite the Heart Foundation and the goal-setters and the financial advisers and my mechanic, there is only one place where peace of mind is found, only one home of happiness. It is the present tense. It is where children and dogs live. And I think we are wise to spend as much time as possible there, even if it means sticking our heads in the sand.

The mechanic has yanked mine out. Damn him, I say.

Food, fun and a tickle behind the ear

Most human beings are docile. They mean no harm and prefer to be left in peace. You and I are likely to get through life without suffering more than a few minor assaults from human beings on our persons or our property. Though there is good reason to be vigilant, there is no reason to be paranoid.

But, as happens every couple of years, events have occurred to inflame paranoia, and the media have cheerfully fanned that flame into a conflagration. It is time to douse it with the hosepipe of reason.

In the process I am not going to gloss over the truth that most attacks on human beings are committed by human beings. Nor am I going to deny that the proportion of viciousness in the human population is higher than in species such as dogs. But I am going to try to restore a sense of proportion.

As anyone who has ever lived with a human being will tell you, by and large they want the same things as you want – food, fun, a tickle behind the ear and as much sex as possible. Millions of human beings, in every part of the globe, offer love and loyalty to their companions and go to their graves having committed no greater sin than gluttony, selfishness or listening to Britney Spears.

That said, it must be noted that the human being is merely a parcel of instincts. Though the parcel comes wrapped in the brown paper and string that we call civilisation, as every postman knows, paper can tear and string fray. And when that happens the instincts poke out and we can get hurt. So it is sensible to understand the beast as well as we can if we are to defend ourselves against him.

The first thing to observe is that the human being is a pack animal. When he joins a pack he becomes a less tractable creature than when he is alone. For evidence one has only to consider parliament, or the crowd at a Britney Spears concert.

The larger the pack the greater the danger. Sometimes a huge pack can form under the leadership of a bellicose lunatic. Such a pack is known as a nation state. The leader rouses the pack by telling them lies and getting them to sing songs full of abstract nouns such as glory, honour and duty. The pack then sets off in formation to attack another pack. These days they send aeroplanes halfway round the planet to drop bombs. The condition is called war, it has recurred throughout human history, and there's not much you can do about it. But at least you get good warning when it's happening.

The human being suffers from delusions. Although few now believe in God – an amusing concept in which human beings created a supreme being in their own image and then insisted it had happened the other way round – most still suffer the hangover from that belief, an inflated sense of their own importance. Torturers, child pornographers, even Britney Spears fans, all take it for granted that they belong to a superior species.

It is true that the human being has a peculiar form of intelligence that has enabled him to make tools. From this has sprung his remarkable expansion across the globe. But at the same time the average human being has never made a tool in his life. The great tools were invented by a few talented and peaceable individuals. The rest of the species has been happy to use those tools and to take the credit by association.

Despite their intelligence, human beings are hard to train. I spent twenty years as a trainer and I'm still not sure how it's done. Nor do I know why a few human beings go bad. The one sure thing is that the damage is done young. It may even occur in the womb. At any rate, by the time a trainer gets to them, it is often too late. And although we no longer destroy vicious human beings, we still rarely cure them.

The other sure thing is that laws don't stop the vicious. They stop only the human beings who don't need stopping. More laws won't prevent more attacks, because human beings who attack already ignore the existing laws. The law can only react.

Some people have argued that control officers should be allowed to enter properties and seize vicious human beings before they attack. The idea is a tempting one, because it is not hard to spot the vicious. At the same time such a law would set a perilous precedent.

So we are left with the problem of how to defend ourselves from attack. A stout stick is useful, but the sort of weapons that would really do the job are illegal except in America. Personally I always carry a loaded Walkman. At the first sign of aggression I turn the volume knob to maximum and press 'play'. It is remarkable to see the instant deterrent effect of *Britney Spears' Greatest Hits*. But perhaps the simplest way, and by far the most pleasant, to defend yourself against the highly unlikely danger of attack by a human being is to get a dog.

Oi Popey-boy

I can't be bothered with interviewing people any more. Most of the people worth interviewing are dead.

But interviews abound. Interviews with pustular rock stars, installation artists, skeletal fashion models, subliterate Hollywood marionettes, quivering novelists with bad breath, footballers.

And the trouble is, of course, that everyone's so flattered to be interviewed that they imagine they must have some thoughts worth attending to and so they spend a day thinking a few up. Then they deliver same with such sonorous earnestness – 'Frankly I see my art works as a search for identity, creating a fusion from the different ways of seeing inherent in our cultural diversity' – that it's all I can do to keep my breakfast down.

Besides it's such a hassle organising an interview, ringing up, say, the Pope and trying to persuade him to nip down to the Volcano for a chat. And then when he does agree there's even more hassle about how to hide security guards behind the Bill Hammonds, what to feed the sniffer dogs, and the exact design of chalice that the Pope's going to swill his Monteiths from, so in the end I always sighingly agree to fly to Rome and to be ushered into the Papal presence as if it were some sort of marquee, a marquee thronged with chubby cardinals and other corporate executives of Him Upstairs. And given the lack of Monteiths and the abundance of circumambient cardinals with ears like tuning-forks, the Pope is always on his best behaviour and simply trots out the party line as laid out in the mission statement sent to all stakeholders a couple of thousand years ago.

So I've resolved to change all that. Henceforth I shall conduct all interviews, as many as three a day, in bed and alone. It's quicker, easier and it gets straight to the truth. Here, for example, is the complete and unedited transcript of the first interview of a series of one, conducted in bed with the Pope shortly after the alarm went off this morning at the crack of ten. It was all over by five past. Efficiency, see.

Me: Oi Popey-boy.

Pope (kneeling, fumbling for a ring to kiss, before I cuff him playfully away): Oh, Your Journalosity. May I say how honoured I am? And with regard to your bid for canonisation . . .

Me: Bid! Let's get this one straight for starters, my preachy pal. When I fancy canonisation I won't be doing any bidding. I'll be instructing. Canonisation, I'll say, and the gun will go off and that will be that. Capisch?

Pope: I'd prefer a flat white.

Me: Coming right up. Meanwhile I've got a short message and I want you to listen up good. You with me?

Pope: Being with you is a privilege, Your Columnness.

Me: Right. Good. Now stop it.

Pope: Stop what?

Me: It. All of it. This religion stuff. It won't do and you know it. It was okay once, laying down the moral law in a lawless time, trying to put an end to the tribal blood feuds and all that (though a glance at the Middle East doesn't suggest much in the way of success) but the point is it just won't wash any more.

Pope: Why are you picking on me?

Me: I'm not picking on you. I've got the rest of them lined up outside this bedroom door right this minute – archbishops, chief moderators, Archimandrites, televangelists, the lot. You just happened to be first because, well, I like you, Popey. I've said so in print before now and I don't retract a word of it, but nevertheless it's time to pull the plug.

Pope: But . . .

Me: But is not a word I'm fond of, Popey-boy. This isn't a discussion. This is an audicncc. So audiate away, my lad of the cloth, and audiate good. I want you to go forth and dismantle the whole shebang. Chasubles, rhythm methods, dog collars, waddling cardinals, the lot. Send it all down the same road as the sun-worship of the Aztecs. I'm not blaming you for all the empire building of the past, for the squillion heathen corpses slaughtered in the name of the boss, for siding with the rich against the poor and all the other ghastlies of yesterday, nor indeed for the retail monstrosity of Christmas, but I am saying that we need to ditch it all now. I mean it's no help when the head honcho of Bushbaby's own church comes out against the war on Iraq on the grounds of scriptural interpretation. Right answer but wrong method. Time to acknowledge, old son, and I know you won't take this the wrong way, the randomness of the world, the pointless atomic structure spinning in a void, and that if we're going to make a go of it we've got to accept there's no authority to fall back on and that it's up to us. All your lot do is cloud the issue. Think comic cosmic irony of purposelessness. Got it?

Pope: Yes.

Me: Good. Now dry your eyes and off you go. Just get out there and sack a few cardinals and you'll feel a whole lot better. Okay?

Pope: Thank you.

Me: A pleasure. Next! Ah, Ayatollah. Come in. Sit down. And listen up.

Shock revelations

In a shock revelation today the formula one world champion explained his success. 'I won because I've got the best car,' he said. 'It goes faster than the other cars and it doesn't break down. If I swapped cars with any of the other guys they'd win.'

When questioned about the shock revelation, a spokesman for the formula one governing body said he didn't know if the champion was telling the truth. 'And to be honest,' he added in a shock revelation, 'I don't care. Our concern is with making money. We do this through sponsorship and advertising and television rights. I have no idea why people want to watch motor racing myself, but as long as they do we're happy to advertise cigarettes and condoms to them.'

A spokesman for the formula one fan club said that he and his friends knew exactly why they liked watching motor racing. 'It's really primitive and stupid,' he said in a shock revelation. 'We like the speed and the noise and the association with glamour and the media hype. Plus there's always the chance of seeing someone killed. That's why we gather at the bends.'

'Death is popular,' confirmed the head of television news in a shock revelation. 'Every day we scour the wires for film of a disaster. The world's a big dangerous place, thank God. We normally find something. Our viewers love it. A good crash is excellent for ratings. That way we can charge more for advertising. Of course if there isn't film of it, it isn't news.'

In response to questioning he agreed that the highlight this week had been the airshow crash in, well, to be honest, he couldn't remember exactly where. 'But that doesn't matter at all,' he said in a shock revelation. 'Our viewers aren't there for information. It was great footage. We ran it four or five times in slow motion.'

'No, I can't remember where the airshow crash happened,' said a spokeswoman for the television news viewers association in a shock revelation, 'but I would like to stress that addicts of the six o'clock news are good conservative people. We think we deplore violence, so we do like to have it presented under the guise of information. It's also comforting to have news readers we like. Somehow we feel we can trust them. Infomercials work on the same principle, you know. That's why people fall for them.'

A fitness instructor confirmed the success of infomercials especially for exercise equipment. 'But,' he added in a shock revelation, rolling up his T-shirt and playing the 'Star-Spangled Banner' on his stomach with a pair of xylophone hammers, 'no one who buys our equipment ever gets abs like mine. In fact we don't expect our exercise equipment to be used for more than a day or two. It's designed to be folded away and forgotten. We have exciting plans,' he added, lowering his voice in a extra shock revelation, 'for a piece of exercise equipment that you don't even have to fold away. It just comes through the post and goes straight under the bed. We're calling it the plankerciser. It's a sure-fire winner. You can sell those suckers anything. We're awash with money.'

'So am I,' agreed a corporate executive in a shock revelation. 'I've got the stuff to burn. It's ridiculous. There's no way I can justify my salary. Every time I look at my pay cheque I just burst out laughing. And as for my automatic bonus – well, words fail me. Surely one day someone's got to realise I'm just a pretty ordinary guy working reasonably hard and that most of my work is straightforward stuff. No one's worth as much dosh as I get.'

In response to questioning he admitted that the gross increase in executive salaries over recent years had begun in the States. 'It's just greed,' he said, in a shock revelation, 'but I guess when you're near the top of the tree there's no one to stop you picking as many peanuts as you fancy.'

When informed that peanuts grew underground he laughed. 'Just goes to show I'm not the sharpest pencil in the box,' he said in a shock revelation. 'But I reckon you get away with what you can.'

'Hear hear,' said a herbalist. 'I mean,' he added in a shock revelation, 'as far as I'm concerned the term herbal remedy is basically an oxymoron. Most illnesses come and go of their own accord, and we herbalists more or less rely on that. But if you contract one of the big nasties that won't go away, you're a damn fool if you take yourself off to the herb garden. You've got as much chance of finding a herbal cure as you have of hearing George Bush admit he screwed up.'

'I screwed up,' said George Bush in a shock revelation.

Ooooh la bloody la

I think,' gushed the woman on the radio in a manner that immediately caused me to doubt the accuracy of the verb, 'I think that France is such a wonderful sensory overload, don't you?'

'No,' I squealed, reaching for the volume control on the radio with a vigour that almost broke the thing off, 'no, I bloody well don't.'

How have the French done it? How have they hoodwinked the world?

Well, let's start where the French start, and where they go on, and where they also finish, which is with food. They are besotted with food, and by and large they cook well. But boy, are they smug about it. Smug and patronising and monomaniac. They are particularly boring about their regional delicacies – the terrine here, the sucking pig there, and, in the region of France where I used to live, the eau de vie de mirabelle. Eau de vie de mirabelle is a liqueur made by infusing the flavours from the small and bitter local plum, the mirabelle, into four-star petrol. The locals talked about it a lot more than they drank it. They also gave it away in tellingly large quantities.

The gushy woman on the radio no doubt finds France a sensory overload because they have outdoor markets where the women sniff melons, squeeze peaches, prod cheeses and generally go to enormous trouble to pass bacteria around. All of which is very picturesque in a touristy sort of way but for one thing it is not unique to France and for another thing I fail to see how it has contributed to the French image of romantic elegance.

For this I suspect we have to look at the language. French, they say, is the language of love. What they mean is that English is the language of love when spoken with a French accent. Why else should all French crooners – from Charles poloneck-sweater Aznavour to that ancient monsieur whose name I've forgotten but who used to knock 'em out with the highly suspect 'Zank heaven for leetle girls' – sing in English? When a Frenchman lays it on, rolling his r's, mispronouncing his th's and throwing the stress onto all ze wrong syllables, every English-speaking woman in a hundred-yard radius goes googly at the knee and subsides into a form of catatonia that disqualifies her from recognising that the average Frenchman is about as romantic as a diesel mechanic from Greymouth.

French itself is a heavily bastardised form of Latin, less mellifluous than Italian, less racy than Spanish and infinitely, but infinitely, less flexible than English. Hence the crusty Académie Française is so terrified of the superior language that for years it has forbidden its citizens, on pain of being pelted to death with petanque balls, to say le weekend. The French, in an unusual display of wisdom, have ignored it.

There is no English Academy. Confident of its own resilience, English has cheerfully absorbed words from wherever it could get them and many have been French. And a remarkable number of these – chic, couture, suave – are associated with style rather than substance.

For somehow the land of berets, bicycles, onions, blue boiler suits, grey plaster houses with grey wooden shutters, straight roads, elm trees that may on reflection be poplars, too many poodles, throat-peeling cigarettes, feeble mopeds and thin beer into which they tip the nauseatingly sweet syrop de grenadine, has become a byword for style and fashion. And as for the notion that the women of France are supposed to be the most beautiful in the world, that stands up to the rigours of close inspection about as well as the notion that it is possible to play rugby against their menfolk without danger to one's testicles.

And then there's Paris. Paris, where fraudulent painters knock up daubs of Montmartre to flog to the tourist dupes and where the most famous building is a giant electricity pylon serving no practical purpose and which was erected in the late nineteenth century as a temporary bit of engineering show-offery. Constantly lauded as the most beautiful city of the world, the city of romance and all the rest of that guff, Paris, like every other European capital, has a fair collection of public buildings – emphatically excluding the Pompidou Centre – but some of the ugliest suburbs in the world, all high-rise sixties monstrosities and streets as mean as Miami.

Yet despite all this, despite the *Rainbow Warrior* and Moruroa Atoll, despite their embarrassing military and imperial record, despite the 2CV and the force-fed geese and the wines that aren't as good as ours, and despite in particular their extraordinary chauvinism – a word derived inevitably from a Frenchman, a Nicolas Chauvin who was ferociously patriotic and devoted in an unhealthy way to that bellicose dwarf Napoleon – France and the French retain a sort of mystique in the Anglo-Saxon mind. Off goes Peter Mayle to Provence to – God, I can hardly bring myself to type this – to do up a farmhouse, and his book sells a squillion copies.

The French are just people like everybody else. They have faults, they have virtues, they have a huge number of myths associated with them and they have a popular fizzy drink called Pshitt.

Wrong room

Last week I stayed in a expensive hotel. Someone else was paying.

The woman at reception programmed a credit card and called it my key. She also gave me a sachet of ground coffee.

On the wall in the lift a picture of a couple in the hotel dining room. She was all blouse and breast. His jaw jutted. Each had a plate of prawns, a glass of white wine and a smile as wide as a bridge.

In the corridor, Muzak, deep carpet and a row of doors like closed eyes. Behind them, no doubt, happy couples preparing to dine. Maids of foreign birth towed carts of sheets and soap and cleaning fluids, and flattened themselves against the wall as I approached.

It didn't take long to open my door with the credit card but the lights in the room didn't work. Because the lights didn't work I couldn't read the telephone instructions. I dialled 1 and spoke to a humming sound. I dialled 9 and spoke to silence. I dialled 0 and spoke to reception.

No, she said in a professional tone that made me feel foolish, of course I wasn't foolish.

When I slipped the credit card into the slot by the door the lights revealed a single chocolate at the head of the bed. While I ate it I read the note from the manager. It wished me happiness and used my Christian name. In search of happiness I opened every cupboard then dialled 0.

No, she said, there wasn't an ashtray because it wasn't a smoking room, and no of course she didn't think me foolish. I agreed to change rooms but didn't mention that I'd eaten the chocolate.

My new room was identical except for an ozone-maker – a metal cube with dials, like the sort of machine that you are supposed to but don't attach to the electricity supply when you're using a hedge trimmer in the rain.

I had to fill the kettle in the bathroom. It fitted awkwardly under the tap. I mopped the floor with two white towels and left them there.

A hotel room is the bed. I took the coffee plunger to the bed, wrestled the pillows from the counterpane, stacked them and folded the top one to support my neck. The bed was aligned inescapably to the television. I flicked through fifteen channels then watched golf. The players wore the same sort of clothes as the jut-jawed man who dined. The caddies wore bibs, like maids.

I would have liked a snack from the mini-bar – peanuts, biscuits, chocolate – but was scared of the prices. At the golf it started raining. The caddies held umbrellas over the players but not over themselves. I pressed the top of the coffee plunger. Coffee spurted over the bedside table and the ozone-maker. I rolled off the bed and fetched a towel from the bathroom then sat on the side of the bed and drank the coffee.

Putting the ironing board up to iron my shirt for the evening was easy. Putting it down again was beyond me. Choosing not to dial 0 I left the ironing board standing.

The bathroom was all mirrors and unguents. Tiny bottles of body lotion and moisturising cream and conditioner and two cakes of pomegranate and honey soap.

Getting the temperature right in the shower took only a few minutes, then I conditioned my armpits and moisturised my crotch. I hadn't closed the shower door properly. I dropped another towel on the floor to soak. While I was drying myself I wiped the condensation from the enormous mirror and did Mr Muscle poses.

I dressed, edged past the ironing board and went out.

I woke in the morning to knocking. A maid, breakfast and a newspaper. I ate in bed, spilling peach juice on my chest and yoghurt on the pillow. I licked the yoghurt off but couldn't reach the peach juice with my tongue. The countless sections of the unfamiliar newspaper dispersed themselves about the bed. On the television, highlights of the golf.

I showered again, using the last of the thousand towels, dressed, gathered my things, made to leave, stopped and surveyed the room that had been home for some fourteen hours. Sodden towels in the bathroom, the bed a stained shambles, the pillows piled haphazardly, the counterpane twisted like a bowel, the breakfast tray lying at a precarious angle, newspaper scattered, the ashtray full, coffee stains on the ozone-maker, the ironing board standing sentinel. Though the place cost $170 a night and was crammed with luxury, it and I had never found a fit. My chin never jutted. I never sipped the white wine, never peeeled the prawns of pleasure.

In the corridor the self-effacing maids were hovering, waiting for me to go, waiting to put things right.

Paper faith

Dismal Philip Larkin, librarian-poet and merchant of dread, whose verse is so exquisitely grim that it curls the hair I haven't got, once wrote that if he were called in to construct a religion he would make use of water. I wouldn't. I would make use of stationery.

Of course the likelihood of my being called in to knock up a religion is negligible. I don't know who does the outsourcing for religion-construction but he's clearly got a predilection for loin-clothed ancients, every one of them a non-smoker. Plenty of cranks have tried to found cults uninvited but they've all turned out to be polygamists, child-botherers or megalomaniacs, keen on the pink Rolls Royce and the self-indulgence stuff but a bit less keen on the self-sacrifice stuff or the thinking stuff or the doing good stuff.

Nevertheless if I did get the summons, I would construct a stationery-based faith. I'm a sucker for stationery. Go into any stationery store and I'm the one staring at the goods in mute adoration while all about me staff with mops and buckets try to stem the flood of my saliva.

Pens. I want all pens. Except felt-tip pens. Felt-tip pens are child's pens, parody pens, all primary colours and too much ink, then suddenly wispy squeakiness and too little. But all other pens and pencils, let them come to me. You can buy ballpoints by the gross. I want to. I want to click their little nipples 144 at a time. I think it was Douglas Adams who identified the point in space where all the unfinished ballpoints come to die. I want to live there.

And ink pens too. Those silver submarines with milled-to-svelteness barrels that nestle in the hand like a sixth finger. Those fluted nibs. A Sunday service would see my acolytes scribbling on the altar. My chalice would be an inkwell, flanked by tooled staplers.

For all the paraphernalia of stationery is manna to me. Paper clips, bulldog clips, manilla folders, those portable concertinas that organise accounts, little boxes of a thousand drawing pins, posh propelling pencils with the fragile twig of graphite – oh my flock, my congregation of inanimate beauty. Even those boxed sets of drawing instruments that grandmothers give to grandchildren at Christmas in the hopeless hope of making Leonardos out of louts, even those are dear. The clear plastic protractor that snaps, the dividers whose purpose I have never understood nestling in their bed of foam, the pairs of compasses whose points draw blood more often than circles. I want them.

But above all it is paper that I love, paper in all its forms. When I was a teacher I hated the photocopier, the hot little room that housed it, the noise it made, its propensity for collapse and the need to probe its mechanical innards. I cursed the surfaces that said 'Caution Hot Surface' and proved against the odds to be hot surfaces. I cursed the last torn fragment of a sheet that stuck between the rollers like gristle in a tooth. I cursed the unsealed toner on the half-finished copy, smudging the hands, soiling the day. But there was one thing I loved about the photocopier. I loved to feed it. I would tear the wrapping from a ream of paper and revel in its heavy flop across my hands. I would riffle the 500 sheets like a croupier for giants. Paper cuts were my stigmata.

Buying for myself I am most drawn to notebooks. Not the spiral kind for keen shorthand reporters, but the bound sort, bound like a book. No picture on the cover, thank you, no cute cartoon, no winsome puppy, no girl on a swing amid lavender. I want leather and tooling. I want books sewn at the spine. I've bought dozens of the things. Most I've never written in.

Why should I love these books? I think that it's the unfulfilment of them, the emptiness and the potential. They offer an invitation. Come on, they say, experience is drifting past you right this minute, lapsing into nothingness at the speed of time. Grasp it. Spread that ink. Form those thin indelible letters. You cannot cup the present in your fingers. Defy the tyranny of time.

And I have tried. I have in front of me a book I bought in Spain in 1979. I used it as a diary. I can see exactly why I bought it – its stout board covers, its stiff straight spine – but how I ruined it with words. The thin mewlings of a self-obsessed youth, the self-pity, the self-dramatisation. It was better blank.

Larkin kept a diary for a while, then stopped. He resolved that if ever he were to start the thing again he should fill it not with thoughts of self but with 'observed celestial recurrences. The day the flowers come, and when the birds go.' Wise man.

Sorry about the stains

ASH are the people who don't like smoking, the habit that a quarter of the population indulges in, and that hastens the death of perhaps a half of that quarter. I'd heard refreshingly little from them in recent months, but a woman from ASH has put an end to that silence. She wants the price of cigarettes to rise. I wrote her name down on a packet of Rothmans, but I've thrown it away, so I'll just call her Wednesday. I felt the need to interview Wednesday.

Thus she becomes the subject of the second of a series of interviews that I am conducting in bed alone. And she may feel encouraged to know that the first of these interviews was with the Pope, so she's in the very best company. Since the publication of that interview, neither the Pope nor any of his tubby cardinals has written to upbraid me, so I can only presume that I represented the Vatican viewpoint with accuracy and sympathy.

Here, then, is the transcript of the interview between me and ASH Wednesday, conducted alone in bed this morning shortly after the lighting of the third gasper following the second cup of Medaglia d'Oro.

Me: Give the dog a nudge and grab a corner of duvet. Sorry about the stains. Smoke?

Wednesday: !

Me: Just my little joke. Oh, what a pretty oxygen cylinder.

Wednesday (waving arms about): !!

Me: Now listen up and listen good. Stop meddling. And just in case you don't understand why, I'm going to explain. I'll start with the little stuff and go on to the big stuff. Ready?

Wednesday does semaphore.

Me: Lovely. Right, the little stuff. Raising the price of fags. First you assert that the price hasn't risen for a couple of years or so. Stop telling fibs. The price rises every six months. By law the government, among whom there is inevitably a hefty proportion of meddlers and wowsers, automatically raises the price of cigs, supposedly 'in line with inflation'. In the last five years the price of cigarettes has risen about 50 per cent. My earnings haven't. The cost of living hasn't. Furthermore, since the price of cigs consists largely of tax, any percentage increase is a tax on a tax. Which pays for more meddling and wowsing. Who'd put up with it but us smokers?

Wednesday gesticulates so wildly that she upsets my coffee.

Me (unperturbed): And who are we? Well, we are mainly the poor. I am not poor, of course. Don't be fooled by the duvet and the cheap mongrel. I am monumentally rich. But most smokers aren't. A lot of them are old men on pensions. They keep smoking. They just eat less and heat themselves less in order to smoke on. They are the government's milch cow. And you want them milched more.

More waving from Wednesday whose message is so transparent that even I, who failed semaphore at naval college, get the idea.

Me: But they don't want to stop. They like it. Leave them be. The tax on their cigarettes has paid for their hospital beds ten times over. Moreover if, as you assert, they're all going to die before their time, well that's a good thing. If your position were even remotely rational you would be urging them to smoke more. More tax to the government, shorter retirements, fewer burdensome old people gone gaga in rest homes, and an end to daytime television. In other words the smoker is an economic and social benefactor of this nation.

Wednesday is now wrestling with her mask but I sweep on.

Me: That's the little stuff. Now the bigger stuff. Do-gooders don't do good. Have a squiz through history and see that that's true. By all means let people know facts. But stop trying to help us. Haven't you got anything else to do? Macramé perhaps? Bulgarian cookery classes? Fishing? Leave us alone. We were never much of a threat to your wellbeing, for all your propaganda to the contrary. Now we're no threat at all. We can't smoke in aeroplanes, offices, cinemas, restaurants. It's easy to stay out of our way. And if you don't like smoky pubs, do as I do with poetry readings.

Wednesday is now battling so vigorously with her mask that the dog wakes from her dream of slow rabbits and stretches luxuriantly.

Me: Like my dog, you and I are mortal beasts. How and when we die is insignificant. If smoke doesn't get us, something else will, and it is likely to be just as nasty. The whole of the commercial world is orchestrated to suggest that we won't die, but it remains the one certainty. I don't expect you to understand this, but some of us resent the sanitised denial of death. And anyway, your warnings about it don't work. In Canada, where they decorate cigarette packets with colour photographs of tumours in a manner that would thrill you to the marrow of your meddling bones, roughly the same proportion of the population still smokes as here.

Wednesday (finally wrenching the mask off): I've seen the light. And the darkness. On my knees I beg forgiveness for my previous meddling.

Me: Good. Smoke?

Wednesday: No thank you. But you carry on.

Artistes and Belgians

The World Cup's been full of surprises. Chief among them has been the Great British hooligan. He's done nothing. Whether he's been influenced by peaceable Japanese society or by the net-guns of the peaceable Japanese police, it is too early to tell. England hasn't lost a game yet.

In the meantime we must look to Russia. The most telling photograph from the adidas-sponsored World Cup was taken in Moscow. It starred a shaven-headed young gallant kicking the bejeebers out of a car. All good clean fun, of course, and an essential part of the grieving process – Russia having just lost to Outer Chad or somewhere – but the neat detail was that the thug was wearing immaculate adidas trainers. The said trainers, moreover, were probably made in Outer Chad by a peasant workforce on half an ounce of UN-provided maize a day, all of which invites earnest comments about globalisation, evil empires and exploit-ative capitalism, none of which I'm going to make because I'm too tired from having sat up all night watching the football.

It's a love fest and everyone loves Brazil. Ronaldo, Ronaldinho, Rivaldo, Rivaldo Junior, they all sound like relatives and when they played Belgium the Great British commentator sounded as though he wanted to marry into the family. 'Rivaldo, not content to meet the ball with his head like a mere mortal, just had to go for the bicycle kick.' The commentator failed to observe that Rivaldo bicycle-kicked the ball thirty feet over the crossbar. When a Belgian, helpfully identified as 'a Belgian', made a better fist of the same manoeuvre the commentator observed that he never really got over the ball.

The Sri Lankan linesman looked terrified of not doing the right thing by Brazil. The referee just got on and did the right thing. When Belgium scored a goal he disallowed it. Replays clearly revealed that he disallowed it for having been scored by a Belgian. The Belgians barely protested. They knew they weren't Brazilians. They just hadn't got it. Their coach looked like a banker. The Brazilian coach looked like ulcers in a polo shirt.

The Brazilians are artistes. It is a short step from artiste to prima donna. Half the Brazilians have already taken that step. So have all the Argentinians. They looked like the cast from *Hair* and played suitably histrionic football. The only time they didn't showboat was when they were eliminated. Then they sat down and wept for real. When they get home the barber will be the least of their worries.

This is the worst-coiffed World Cup in history. The black Belgian centre forward led the way with the Oprah Winfrey look, while David Beckham went for the white-tipped mohawk. Beckham's got an educated boot but a pig-ignorant stylist. He looks like a cockatoo in baggy shorts.

All Japanese people have got black hair unless they play football for their country. Then they've got hair like Beckham. Having only recently latched on to football the Japanese are imitating best practice. It would be unwise to mock them. Thirty years ago the Japanese had only recently latched on to electronics.

If economic history is any guide, Japan will win the World Cup inside twenty years. At the time of writing they could even win this one. If so, watch for some imitative hooliganism. Done very politely in adidas trainers.

Apart from their hair and hooligans, the English lack flair. They make up for it with phlegm. Their chief phlegmatist is a Swedish coach whom the Belgians rejected as too conventional. He gives vent to extreme emotion by nudging his spectacles up his nose. When Beckham comes back from the barber he nudges them down again.

The Swedish team all wore their hair in a manner that suggested that they wanted to be Belgian coaches. They lost to the most intriguing team present, Senegal. The Senegalese have got a lot to learn about hair but they play exquisite football. I've been informed that Senegal lies between Mauritania and Guinea-Bissau. That doesn't help much, but they're the only team who celebrate a goal in a manner that doesn't induce a cringe.

Part of the joy of African football lies in the names. The Senegalese strikers are called, if memory serves, Camera and Papa Joop. Another African team fielded Justice and Yobbo. The Swedes were all called Something Somethingsson. They never stood a chance. But it was predictably Belgium who reached rock bottom. They brought on a substitute called Wesley Sonck.

Because it's played by national teams, the World Cup offers a more accurate microcosm of the globe than the Olympics do. And all the evidence suggests that Asia and Africa are the rising stars and that Europe's lost its zest. And as the old order changeth, everything from hair to hooligans is wonderful fun to watch.

Into a briar bush

I don't know the gentleman's name but it would be pleasant and uplifting to introduce myself to him. And here is how I'd do so. I would extend my hand and as he extended his I would seize him by the genitals, and swing him, say, four or five times around my head in the manner of a hammer thrower. The anonymous gentleman would, I fancy, be too surprised to squeal.

And having swung him in circles of deliciously increasing radius I would toss him in a looping parabola, in the manner of whoever it was that tossed Brer Rabbit into a briar bush. Of course Brer Rabbit was eager to be tossed into the briar bush because he felt at home in briar bushes, but I am confident that my victim would not feel so at home. Being pallid, craven and undoubtedly urban, his skin would turn to bloody ribbons at the first thorny kiss of the briar. Furthermore I would ensure that this particular briar bush consisted not only of briar but also of gorse, nodding thistle, scotch thistle, teasel, cleavers (commonly known as goosegrass) and an abundance of ferocious stinging nettle. Were the briar bush also to contain a small stand of the venomous hemlock, known, with a neatness of irony that I would take pains to point out to him, as Mother Die, I wouldn't complain. With his screams echoing through the valley but reverberating in no sympathetic ears I would go away to wash my hands and leave him to battle the vegetable armoury in solitude.

My reason? Well, imagine, if you would, the hills of Southern England some forty years ago. Look closely at your mental picture and you will note a child with hair the colour of marigolds, prancing across the springy turf and clutching in his hand a piece of vegetation. Cup your ear and listen to his needle squeak.

'O Mother dear,' he squeaks, 'do look at this. I'm sure I've found at last a specimen of that elusive rarity the hoary buntwort.'

His mother wears a sixties summer frock of gaily printed cotton. She takes the vegetation, glances at it, gently shakes her head.

'The sepals, dear,' she says, 'just look at the sepals.' And the boy's head slumps and he doesn't look at the sepals because he's already looked at them. He knows that those sepals are dentate rather than auricular, and that what he's brought his mother was never going to be the hoary buntwort but only its abundant common cousin the mouse-eared buntwort.

But off the boy scampers once again to scour the ground. Next time perhaps he brings a plant to Mother and she stops and looks at it and says, 'Well now, what have we here?' And then she tucks it in a pocket on her skirt and takes it home. And later on that day she takes down from the shelves a hefty book of wild flowers, and with her son agog at her side she compares the wilting specimen with pictures in the book and reads the paragraph about the plant in question, and says, 'Why yes, I thought as much, the spiny hawk-bit.' And then she takes a ballpoint pen and puts a tick beside the picture of the spiny hawkbit and notes the date and place where it was found.

That prancing boy was me. That mother, unsurprisingly, was mine. Her knowledge of the wild flowers of the hills and lanes and hedgerows is compendious. Lady's slipper, cuckoopint, birdsfoot trefoil, the campions, both red and white, the endless different types of vetch, all these and hundreds more are stamped within my mother's mind as sweet familiar companions, recurrent annual symbols of the cycle of the seasons.

And all those flowers are ticked and dated in her book, the book she's owned for forty-something years. And just as wine laid down matures and gathers character, so my mother's flower book has slowly changed in nature. What started as a work of reference has become something personal. It reads like poetry. What seemed mundane when written – Butcher's Wood, September '63, Ditchling Beacon, July '71 – reads like an alternative and better history to the one that finds its way into official books, the one that is accepted as the truth about the time we lived in.

The book itself has worn. Its spine is crumbling. Many of the pages are held in place by sticky tape, tape that time has made brittle and yellow. But the book has endured and held the past within its covers.

Until, that is, quite recently, when someone whose name I'll never know broke into my mother's car and stole the book. And it is that someone, of course, that I would cheerfully toss among the briars, just as he no doubt tossed the book aside when he found it had no monetary value.

It doesn't matter much, I suppose, but still it seems to me a violation. And I would relish the chance to violate back.

The juiciness

Is there better? There is not. Now is spring and it's in the bones. The land has taken off its thick brushed-cotton pyjamas and is risking its baby flesh.

The kowhai's covered in drab little fat things, khaki in colour, things that will burst tomorrow or the next day into dragon-tongue flowers. Why? Who knows? Who cares? 'Earth's immeasurable surprise', as dismal old Larkin put it, stirred from his bang-true suburban dreariness for once to toast the juiciness of spring.

The cherry tree I never prune and from which I've never had a cherry because the chaffinches, greenfinches, starlings, silver-eyes, blackbirds, sparrows, thrushes assault it on the very day of ripeness and strip the flesh to dangling stones, is a globe of blossom, whiter than my laundry, than your laundry, than advertising laundry. It's stopping-to-stare white.

Seven in the morning, and so that I can see the screen of this computer I've half-drawn the blind beside my desk against the rising sun. The bald plastic side of the machine is tiger-striped with sunshine. My hands on the keyboard move in and out of bars of light and my skin registers the faint heat. The air is still as expectancy. And yet last night the wind blew wild from the west. It flipped the lid from the dustbin and tossed it somewhere else. Throughout the night the wind wiped the great dry brushes of the gum tree across the iron of my roof. It whipped the street-trex – the wrappers, leaves and advertising pamphlets – into eddies and dumped it in corners. It sprinkled the dog's water bowl with dust and spent, papery blossom. Then just before dawn it went away and left the morning faultless.

The daffs are pretty well done, their frilly loud-hailers gone ragged, edged with brown, but they have handed over yellow like a relay baton to the persistent pestilential broom. All over the hills behind my house the broom has pushed out shoe-and-wimple flowers the colour of fresh butter.

My hens feast on dandelions and hawkweed, ripping at the translucent vegetable flesh with quick and vicious pincer beaks, intent on selfishness. The dandelions and hawkweed keep on thrusting, undissuaded, equally intent. I'm overwhelmed with eggs, their yolks the colour of yesterday's daffs, today's broom, tomorrow's kowhai.

A southerly's due this afternoon. The delicate stuff of spring will sit it out, tough in its delicacy, choiceless.

My dog basks on the deck, no longer curled against the winter, but unfurled, stretched, absorbent, her black fur gleaming and hot as an oven.

In town the lunchtime jackets will dangle over shoulders from single looped fingers. Ties will loosen and people will laugh at outdoor tables over beer that will grow tepid in the toe-end of the glass. Windscreens, blocked with folding Japanese screens of cardboard, will flash singly. In the supermarket carpark even the stunted town-planner trees will feel the suck of sap from underneath the chipped bark and the asphalt and will droop less. The synthetic colours of the shop windows will wilt in the shade.

Last year my neighbour down below painted part of the side of his house. All winter I have overlooked a weatherboard wall that's one-third pink and two-thirds turquoise. This morning maybe he will stop and look and remember, and this evening he'll think scrapers and brushes. The roof he cannot see could do with his attention. The rust grows rich in the sun. The iron expands. And along the ridge line dance distorting wraiths of heat, the first ghosts of summer. A starling perches momentarily, feathers shimmering like puddled petrol.

Soft bare feet on hard warm concrete, I pad down the steps to fetch the morning paper. Green and nameless plants, the plants you won't find in the garden centre, are pushing up through every crack in the concrete of my drive. If I do nothing about them they'll eventually win, lifting the drive into lumps, tipping it slowly over into rubble and then smothering it. I must let loose the chooks.

The rolled paper is warm, the cellophane wrapper pudgy. The front page is all war. The simple-minded bumbler in the White House wants to sock it to the despot over there. He wants a head on a stake to wave before his people. The head he really wants he can't get, so he goes for another. Propaganda scraps with propaganda on the printed page. Beside the words and dwarfing them, a picture of a Stealth bomber, all blackly beautiful destructive genius, born in the winter of the heart. The dog and I are going out.

And let him hate you

Do you know *The Midnight-Skaters* by gentle Edmund Blunden? Well, nor did I until this morning.

The poem tells the story, astonishingly, of skaters at midnight. Their rink is a pond. They don't know how deep the pond is, nor how thick the ice, but still the damned fools skate. I discovered the poem because of ACC.

Like all the self-employed I relish getting letters from ACC. Most of them ask for money and I pay with a song in my heart. My ballpoint dances as I write a cheque for about 3 per cent of my annual income after tax, because I know that by doing so I'm not only insuring myself against the danger of tumbling headlong into my keyboard, but that I'm also paying for those who have tumbled before me. Not a sparrow falls into its iMac, as the Bible puts it, but ACC sees it fall, and catches it, and cradles it, and lugs it off to hospital to make it better.

So though my ACC insurance costs three times as much as the combined insurance for my house, its contents and my big red dirty car, I pay cheerfully through both nostrils.

And there I thought the matter rested. But then yesterday ACC sent me a new sort of letter, a letter that thrust responsibility upon me. This is a partnership, they said, and we want you to stand beside us, man and bureaucracy, shoulder to shoulder. Are you up for it? they asked. Oh golly yes, I said.

So from 5 May this year I have new responsibilities, and here, in ACC's own honeyed words, is the first and the best of them.

'You have a responsibility to record all work-related injuries, illnesses and near-misses that occur . . . The necessary details can be recorded in a book that you keep with your first-aid kit.'

Well, as you can imagine, it was the work of a moment to stash an exercise book behind the scotch bottle. But it didn't stay there long. Because ACC had opened my eyes, and once opened they proved hard to close. I found myself reviewing the near-misses of my self-employed life. Down came the exercise book and out came the pencil. And I was away.

6.30 a.m. Fetching the paper from the wet drive in the darkness, wearing jandals and a dressing gown, is the action of a reckless fool. How close I must have come a thousand times to slipping, falling, clutching at nothing and shattering my teeth against the unforgiving concrete. Henceforth I'll be aware that danger lurks in every crevice of this mortal world, and when I go to fetch the paper of a morning I shall wait until the day has broken, I shall limber up before I tackle steps so cruelly precipitous, I shall wear safety footwear, and, in case the dreaded accident should still oc- cur, as it so clearly could, I shall carry with me on my expedition into peril, a cellphone, fully charged and pre-set with the numbers of the fire brigade, police and ambulance, and also ACC.

Memo to self – buy cellphone.

And that was just the start. I'd been out to feed the chickens without a thought to vaccination against coccidiosis. When I took the dog to romp about the hills, I left no note to say where we had gone. Nor did I carry crampons, high protein rations for myself and dog or even an emergency locater beacon.

By the time that kindly providence had brought me safely home and I had drunk – oh God, I shudder to think of it – a vat of caf- feine-laden coffee, and smoked three cigarettes, and still, though God alone knows how, clung on to life, I found that I had written half a dozen pages crammed with glimpses of the abyss, and my nerves were shot.

So I sought solace, as I often do, in verse, and it was then I came across old Blunden. In one way ACC would like him. For Blunden was aware that in the black depths of the pond on which the skat- ers skated, there lurked death. 'What wants he but to catch,' asks Blunden, 'earth's heedless sons and daughters?' To which ACC would say the heartiest 'indeed'.

But in the final stanza Blunden goes all wrong. Instead of urging the skaters off the ice and into the safety of an air-conditioned mall to buy some thermal underwear and leave nasty old death alone, Blunden advises them, believe it or not, to taunt death.

> Then on, blood shouts, on, on,
> Twirl, wheel and whip above him
> Dance on this ball-floor thin and wan,
> Use him as though you love him;
> Court him, elude him, reel and pass,
> And let him hate you through the glass.

I hope, when they finished skating, they made a near-miss entry.

Hope is dead

Shoot the astrologers. Burn the tarot cards. I'll give you a glimpse round time's corner myself.

No need even to cross my palm with low-denomination banknotes – though a little gin money is always welcome in this cruel weather. Behold, for nothing, courtesy of my generous disposition, the future.

But before you behold, beware. It is dangerous to know the future. All who've peeped at it – Oedipus, Faust and many another sadsack – have come to ends so sticky you could mend furniture with them. Better to turn the page now. Stay ignorant and happy.

If you choose to keep reading, the risk is yours. You've been warned. And if, on some distant morning, you wake to foam-rubber decor and electrodes on your temples, well, don't come bleating to me.

Soppy to the core, we imagine the future will be nice. The future means winning the jackpot of happiness. The future means chance encounters with beautiful strangers who immediately stop being strangers and take their clothes off. Experience tells a different story, of course, but we all prefer the fantasies of hope.

Well, hope is dead. Take my hand and I will show you the way the world is going.

I have a friend whom I'll call Adam. He works for the government. Adam has recently been posted to a Pacific Island. And there, despite the twanging ukuleles and the languorous lagoons and the soporific heat and the feathery palms and the phosphorescent fish, Adam chooses not to lounge on the beach sipping drinks with umbrellas in. He goes running. The lounging locals stare at Adam with the sort of detached amusement with which Elizabethans stared at the mad.

Wild dogs infest the island. They stare at Adam with a less detached amusement. Apparently these dogs live on crabs. And the dogs see Adam as a dietary supplement. Adam is understandably alarmed. Knowing I know something of dogs, Adam sought my advice.

I wrote Adam a substantial email. I told him of a Victorian vicar who always carried a coat and an umbrella. If a bad dog approached, the vicar draped the coat over the umbrella and shoved it at the dog. The dog seized the coat. This positioned the dog nicely for the vicar to swing his boot and collect the dog under the chin. Ungodly but effective.

I wrote plenty more such helpful stuff, including a cheerful description of a removal man I once saw bitten on the buttocks by a dog. Then I pressed 'send'. But the email did not reach Adam. The government sent it back to me.

For all I know, at this very moment and for want of my advice, Adam may be down on the sand beside the languorous lagoon being mauled to death by wild dogs, while the locals look on with detached amusement, strumming their ukuleles and taking care not to stab themselves in the eye with a drink umbrella. If so, blame the government. Or more specifically, blame MailMarshal.

Because MailMarshal intercepted my email to Adam, read it, went puce around the gills, and sent it back with a note attached. It was a curt note. No 'dear' at the start. No parting benison of love or kisses.

Here is what Mailmarshal wrote:

MailMarshal (an automated content monitoring gateway) has stopped the email for the following reason:

It believes it may contain unacceptable language, or inappropriate material.

Please remove any inappropriate language and send it again.

Script Offensive Material Triggered
Expression: (my OR your OR nice OR big OR the OR her OR his OR fat OR tight OR sweet OR great) FOLLOWED BY 'arse'

And there we have it. Behold tomorrow in all its unglory. Told off by a machine. A machine, furthermore, that is not subject to its own rules. I sent it a mild vulgarity. It sent me back a note so suggestive, so crammed with boggling sexual possibility, that I had to lie down and fan myself with a dog-eared copy of the *Norwegian Naturist*.

Once I'd recovered I set to work on MailMarshal. To find out where it drew its lines, I sent it screeds of emails. It accepted gluteus maximus. It accepted bum, buttocks, bottom, situpon, posterior, rectum and jacksie. But it turned down, well, let's not worry about what it turned down.

In a final provocative torrent I sent Mailmarshal a note using every one of the offending words it sent me, and more than a few of my own, a note so rich that it would have shivered the timbers of my nautical great-uncle Dick. MailMarshal has yet to reply.

But it will. Machines persist. They know no better. MailMarshal will carry on long after the death of the prurient bureaucrat who programmed it. Indeed, long after Adam's bones have been bleached to the colour of the sand they may be lying on, long after Baghdad has been razed to rubble, long after, indeed, the human race has poisoned or bombed itself into holes in the ground, MailMarshal, son of MailMarshal, and a host of other 'content monitoring gateways' will be protecting us from naughty words, imposing arbitrary illiterate primness on words sent from friend to friend.

Automated censorship. You read it here first.

In and out

The Department of Corrections has corrected me.

Some weeks ago I wrote an article about the lousy library at Paparua Prison. I was acting on information received. When the prison authorities read the article, they invited me to visit and receive some different information.

The morning was exquisite, the sky above the plains as wide as freedom, and as blue and delicate as a starling's egg. In front of the prison a tractor ploughed a paddock. With the recent rains the turned earth shone like polished chocolate. But the inmates couldn't see it. Two 6-metre fences stood between them and it, two sets of mesh blurring every image of the world beyond. The fence tops glinted with razor wire.

Just inside the fences a tall gum tree grew. I imagined myself escaping, shinning up the tree at three in the morning, tossing a prison-issue blanket over the razor wire, dangling, dropping, then stumbling frantically across the ploughed paddock. In my mind I heard a siren wailing, guards shouting, dogs barking, and the director saying 'cut'. Because, apart from two adolescent nights in police cells, my images of prison are drawn from films or books. They are romantic images. Paparua Prison is not a romantic place.

The entrance block looks like an airport terminal. But there are grilles over the windows, a sign saying prams will be searched, and a plaque announcing that the building was opened by Matt Robson. I suppose that ministers must love those plaques. The Christ's College library has a plaque announcing that it was opened by Prime Minister Geoffrey Palmer. If I remember rightly, Geoffrey

Palmer was prime minister for seven and a half minutes. I wonder how many plaques he notched up.

I was taken to the governor whose office was like, well, any office. There was a photocopier and people carrying files, and a round coffee table at which I sat but got no coffee. Instead I was told some good statistics which I didn't doubt, and some bad ones which I didn't doubt either. I learned that many inmates reoffended but that they were less likely to reoffend if they discovered their roots, a woman, or God. I learned how every inmate's needs were judged, and his sentence planned to meet those needs. And while I discussed these things with free men and women, I was aware that I was nervous of heading into the prison proper. I would feel like a voyeur.

Two warm and twinkly librarians took me down corridors that smelt of disinfectant and crackled with testosterone. It was like a boys' boarding school, except that the corridors were repeatedly blocked by floor-to-ceiling metal gates. A camera scrutinised us and then the gates swung slowly open like the heavy doors to bank vaults.

I had written that the library held few books. I was wrong. It holds no books. This is partly because the inmates kept stealing them, but mainly because the building is condemned. It would fall down in an earthquake. The librarians are waiting for a new building. I wanted to say that I would fall down in an earthquake too, but that didn't stop me owning books. But I didn't say it.

The librarians took me down more and worse corridors to where the books are stored. They called the place The Black Hole. It was not a big room and there weren't that many books. Money, they said, was short.

Nevertheless the inmates have unlimited access to books. They can order anything they like, and the librarians will acquire it through the public library system.

But some inmates can't read. And many just don't. Although the librarians do what they can to advertise their service, only about 15 per cent of inmates use it. And some of those deface the books. I was shown a big book with a picture cut neatly out of it.

The book was an illustrated history of crime.

Not long ago an inmate who'd completed his sentence tried to leave with two stolen books. One was a Maori dictionary. The other was a Harry Potter. The authorities took the books away. I said it would have been good if they had let him keep them. Yes, said the librarians, but they would soon run out of books.

In the North Island an organisation called Books in Prisons distributes books that inmates can keep. The scheme has yet to come south.

I spent two hours in the prison and met both staff and inmates. I liked almost all the people I met. But the difficulties of the prison library are the difficulties of prison itself.

Prison is contradictory. It exists to punish, but it aims to rehabilitate. It stands beyond the city walls, but it hopes to fit people back into the city. Punishment and education sit awkwardly together, as any teacher who has ever taken Friday night detention will tell you.

There's a lot to say about crime and punishment and I'm told that Dostoievski said it. All I can say is that when I left the prison, the paddock had been ploughed and the tractor had gone. And it felt good to get out.

Unreal

Dorothy and I only ever wanted to be on reality television. Without it life seemed unreal.

And we tried. God knows we tried. We applied to change rooms. We applied to live in a gated community. We applied to auction our house, to survive in the bush, to rip up our garden, to live in Victorian conditions. We applied for every reality going. They turned us down.

Condemned to unreal, untelevised lives, we drifted without purpose. 'Is this real?' I would say of my toast every morning, and I'd look around the kitchen for the cameras.

But it was Dorothy who suffered most. She sank into a depression so severe it seemed almost real. I had to snap her out of it.

'Dorothy,' I said, one particularly grim morning, 'let's do it ourselves. DIY reality.'

'You mean . . .'

'Yes, let's pretend. Let's do our own virtual-reality reality. It might not be the real thing but we've got to face, well, facts.'

'But what about, you know, the stuff?' said Dorothy. 'The cameras, the vacuous bimbos, the interior designers, the hyperbolic commentators, the artificial storyline – they're beyond us.'

'Nothing's beyond us, Dorothy, my love,' I said.

That day I resigned from my job. The boss didn't understand. He kept saying, 'This is the real world, Peter.'

I came home with two video cameras, a heap of plywood and a blow-up doll. 'Hey presto,' I exclaimed, as I put the foot pump to the doll and her head filled with air. 'Our very own bimbo.'

'Perfect,' said Dorothy, 'just perfect. Impossible to tell from the real thing. Oh Peter,' and there was a light in her eye I hadn't seen for months, 'I'm really happy.'

'Really?'

'Really and truly,' she said, then checked herself. 'Well, virtually really. Oh Peter, I do love you. You're my very own big brother.' And she hugged me with a tenderness that we both mistook for the real thing.

I pushed her away and handed her a camera. 'No more of that,' I said, 'this is survival. From now on we're on our own.'

We divided the house with the plywood. I let her have the kitchen. I didn't care about food. I wanted things reality tough. At the same time as surviving we would each redcorate a room.

Rigging the camera in a corner, I set to work. Down came the wallpaper, the pelmets, the plaster arch, the bookcase full of fiction. No fiction here any more. We were living a non-fiction life. I stripped the floor back to its original boards. There were no original boards. I stripped the floor back to bare earth. Funky.

With the room stripped I went out to buy nails, creosote and a second-hand zebra skin. I got the lot for a song. The song was the one I had planned for *Stars in Their Eyes*. I didn't need it any more.

Back home I nailed up the front door. No everyday fantasy would intrude on our reality. I stripped the sofa and recovered it with the zebra skin. I creosoted the wall for that contemporary sticky, textured feel. On the earth floor I made a campfire out of old wallpaper and filmed myself sitting round it, impaling fleas from the zebra skin on a furniture tack, toasting them till they popped, then eating them. They tasted bad. Survival bad. Real bad. I took charcoal from the fire and smeared my face. It looked good. Survival good. Real good.

Now all I needed for the programme was conflict. I would raid Dorothy's kitchen. I waited till midnight. Then masked, bandannaed, warpainted, with a remnant of zebra skin over my shoulder, I took down the plywood partition and found myself on enemy territory. The old kitchen had never seemed so real.

Suddenly the light came on. In front of me an apparition I still struggle to describe. Its wrists seemed to have snapped. Its fringe of hair flopped with a loose insouciance. It wore studiedly torn jeans, an aura of smugness and a single earring. It made to kiss me. I screamed. I screamed and I screamed. I screamed for real.

'Darling,' the apparition shouted, 'darling, Peter, it's me, Dorothy. I'm not really an interior designer. Darling, it's all right. You'll survive. Really.'

It was then that the police broke down the door. Apparently the neighbours had called. They'd been watching the house. A crowd had gathered. As an ambulance man led me out I saw a man toting, could it be, yes, a TV camera.

'That's not a . . .' I said.

'Yeah, mate,' said the ambulance man. 'Want a blanket over your head?'

I smiled.

'Unreal,' I said. And they led me away.

Exactly, yes, me too

On a scale from one to ten, how nice are you? Exactly, yes, me too. If there were more people like us the world would be, well, nicer.

In my abundant niceness I was sitting outside Wellington airport. I was brushing my teeth and reading a book called *Cod*. It was about cod. Apparently cod sustained the slave trade. Dried and salted cod was a cheap way of keeping slaves alive in the West Indian sugar plantations. The plantation owners paid for the cod with molasses. The molasses went to make rum. The slaves didn't get any rum. They got sixteen hours work a day cutting sugar cane, cod for dinner and an early death. Nice.

I was brushing my teeth to try to dislodge a piece of Origin Pacific salami. It had wedged itself between two back left lower molars. My tongue could do nothing with it. Hence the toothbrush. Had I been in the main street of Lyttelton I would have been too nice to use the toothbrush. But in the anonymity of Wellington I felt free to do so.

A car pulled up. It was a big executive-type car with tinted windows. A big executive-type man got out and locked the car with one of those remote beeper things that make the park-lights flash so that everyone can see you've got one of those remote beeper things. Then he hurried into the airport through the sort of automatic glass doors that open fractionally slower than you want them to.

A notice stood on the forecourt anchored against the wind. It said that this was a drop-off zone and unattended vehicles would be clamped or towed away 'at the owners expense'. It was a strong notice that did not bother with apostrophes. It was the sort of notice that nice people like us obey and executive-type people ignore.

I had noticed the notice but I did not draw it to the executive-type's attention. Instead I lowered my toothbrush and looked around in hope.

A youth emerged from the airport with a yellow fluorescent jerkin, enormous shoes and a walkie-talkie. I urged him to notice the car. He noticed the car. He walked around it. He peered through its tinted windows. He spoke into his walkie-talkie. I couldn't hear the words but I knew exactly what I wanted them to be.

The youth went back inside. I worried that the executive-type would return and unbeep his car and drive away. The doors opened and I turned to look and the youth reappeared. He was carrying a clamp. 'My heart leaps up,' wrote Wordsworth, 'when I behold a rainbow in the sky.' I felt the same way about the clamp.

The youth dithered. He scanned the forecourt. He spoke again into his walkie-talkie. He toured the car again. I suspected that he was a nice youth, and a slightly frightened one. Nice and frightened are often the same thing.

Then he clamped the car. I marked my page in *Cod* and put the book away. I had better things to attend to.

I had my car clamped once, ten years or so ago in Earls Court in London. To pay to have the clamp removed I had to go to an underground bunker. It was the angriest place I have ever been. The air was soup-thick with anger. Cashiers sat behind grilles of tiger-grade zoo mesh. When I saw how angry everyone else was I tried not to be angry. I tried to be nice to the woman who took my money. She was not used to nice.

And now I waited for the executive-type to emerge and get angry. I half hoped he would assault the youth. If he did I would leap up like Wordsworth's heart and restrain him. Perhaps I would whack him round the head a bit with *Cod*, or jab him with my toothbrush. I often have such fantasies, leaping to fight for a cause. I have yet to act on one. The executive-type did not emerge. I looked at my watch. Time drags in airports, but now it was sprinting. I was almost due to board my plane.

A woman sat beside me and lit a cigarette and sighed. She worked in an airport shop. She said it was good to take the weight off her feet for a few minutes. I pointed at the car. 'That bloke's been clamped,' I said.

'Oh good,' she said.

'That's not very nice,' I said.

She turned quickly to look at me, to judge my tone. I smiled and then we both laughed.

'I hope he hurries up,' said the woman. 'I've got to go back to work soon.'

'I've got to catch a plane,' I said, and I did. On the plane I managed to dislodge the salami with my finger.

Is there anybody there?

*W*hen I heard that the government had raised the excise tax on
light spirits and fortified wines in order to separate the young
from the stomach-pumps, I knew immediately that the story was
beyond my scope. It called for someone who knew what was what
with adolescence, so I rang Enid Blyton.

Her housekeeper informed me that the mistress had been a bit
quiet these thirty-five years on account of an attack of jolly old death
but if I cared to leave a message . . . I rang off. I knew what I had
to do.

It was the work of a minute to scatter Scrabble pieces on the side
table, place a wine glass upside down in their midst and drape the
lot in a suitably eerie ambience. Enid's finger might be skeletal but I
was confident it remained on the pulse of youth affairs and capable
of tapping out a moral yarn that would say all that needed saying
on the matter.

Within seconds the ouija glass was skidding like a boy racer. And
here are the skid marks.

The Famous Five Go Binge-Drinking
By a shade purporting to be that of Ms Blyton

'I say, George,' said Dick, 'it's Saturday night. Let's go out and get
completely. . .oh damn it.'

'Dick,' exclaimed George, 'what's the matter?'

'Dash it and golly,' said Dick sucking his finger. 'I've stabbed
myself with the darning needle.'

'You silly thing, Dick,' said Anne reprovingly. 'But if you will go trying to lower the crotch of your skateboard trousers without wearing a thimble, what do you expect? Here, give them to me. Now just sit yourself down and George will get you a sherry.'

'Here you are, Dick,' said George. 'That'll put hairs on your chest.'

'Sherry's antiseptic, isn't it?' said Dick, plunging his finger into the glass and swirling it around so that blood mingled with the sun-soaked sweetness. But George was looking at Dick with horror.

'What's the matter, George?' said Dick. 'There's plenty more where that came from.'

'No Dick, there isn't. That's the last of the amontillado and the Dubonnet gave out last week.'

'Well, waste not want not,' said Dick, knocking back the crimson glass in a single swig. 'Whew, that's what I call a Bloody Mary. But don't worry George, I'll take Timmy the dog for a drive down to the bottle store in my $20,000 saloon car with the boombox that gave Julian renal damage, and we'll just flash the fake ID you bought in the Square and . . .'

'But Dick,' exclaimed George, 'you silly ass. Haven't you been listening to the radiogram? The grown-up government has just increased the tax on the fortified wines that we've been getting so jolly blotto on every night.'

'Nonsense,' exclaimed Dick. 'They can't. Everyone knows that we're below the legal drinking age. The government can't tax illegal drinking. They'd be taxing crime. And that amounts to living off immoral earnings.'

'O Dick,' said Julian, 'if your liver holds out you really ought to think about being a lawyer when you grow up. You're so frightfully clever. But all the same it's true what George says.'

'Well, I think this needs investigating,' said Dick. 'Is anybody up for an adventure?'

'You bet we are,' said everybody except for Timmy the dog who just barked, so Dick, Julian, George and Anne put on their having-an-adventure clothes and Timmy the dog put on the muzzle that the grown-up government required him to wear when outdoors and the Famous Five set off to Parliament.

'We may need this,' said Dick, brandishing half a dozen sticks of gelignite.

'Oh what fun,' said Julian.

As they bicycled into town they passed a long queue of traffic all heading towards Wellington airport. 'Who are all these people?' asked George.

'Well,' said Julian, 'some of them are old people who like a sherry of an evening, others are winemakers and the rest are smokers or dog-owners. They're all emigrating because . . .'

'Shh,' said Dick, 'we're here.' Before them stood the grey walls of Parliament. 'Come on,' said Dick and before they knew it they were in a shrubbery outside a window. By standing on tip toe they could see into a room where a group of very serious grown-ups were sitting round a table. On the table stood a model of a yacht with the names of several companies on the hull including a brewery.

'So,' said a waspish little man in spectacles, 'the increased excise tax will fund the bowsprit and the bailing bucket, but as for. . .' and then he stopped because Timmy the dog had ripped off his muzzle, seized the bundle of high explosives, leapt through the window, tied up all the grown-ups, lit the fuse, paused to widdle on the yacht and jumped back out of the window into the waiting arms of Dick.

'Run,' screamed Julian. And they all ran like billyo and dived through the door of The Backbencher as the blast rattled the windows.

'Well done everybody,' said Dick. 'And especially you, Timmy. This calls for sherry all round.'

'Woof woof,' said Timmy the dog.

No children litter the step

In sepia snaps of early nineteenth-century New Zealand, settlements consist of wooden shacks with corrugated roofs and sprawls of dusty grinning urchins in the street outside. But in among the fragile penetrable buildings stand two more solid ones of brick or masonry, like sound teeth in a rotting mouth. One's the church. The other is a four-square double-storey thing. Its windows are small and grilled, its title etched in plaster round the pediment. Its doors are flanked by Graeco-Roman columns. No children litter its step. It is the bank.

Banks do simple business. They borrow money at a certain rate and lend it at another. The difference between the two buys window-grilles and plaster pediments and suits as dull as Sunday.

Banks are adult. Banks are sober. Banks are austere. And banks are necessary. We hold them in our minds, as we do most authorities, in double guise. We depend on them and yet we like to dislike them.

Few children aspire to banking. It doesn't cut a dash. It is the embodiment of prudence. Prudence, said Blake, is a rich, ugly, old maid courted by incapacity. But banks are capable.

Inactive things themselves, they put their money out to people who are active, people who will do and make things. In exchange banks take a slice of profit. Effectively banks gamble. Admittedly they gamble on as close to racing certainties as they can find, but a punt remains a punt. Yet though we love a punter, it's hard to love a bank.

Banks call their services products, but they lie. They produce nothing but profits. They trade in money and money is not a thing in itself, but rather a medium, an image of things. You can't eat it. You can't build or hunt or grow things with it. You can't fight with it. Take a million bucks into the bush and see what it's worth. It makes reasonable but short-lived kindling.

We feel ambiguously towards money. We love the stuff because of its wad-weight of promise, the potential for delight that it holds within its sexy numbers. But we also despise it. We talk of being filthy rich. We talk of rolling in it. Money has a strange totemic quality, a religious aura. We are shy of openly discussing it. We speak of it in euphemisms, just as we do of God or sex. Money becomes funds, revenue streams, allocations.

That same ambivalence extends to banks. Though most of us choose to use a bank and readily accept the interest that it pays, and the loan that it extends to help us buy a house, we universally resent the fees it charges for the work it does, and the way that it protects itself from loss. We see it somehow as a parasite upon our industry. And we resent it as we resent anything to which we are indebted.

We don't like bank robbers but only because they terrify the workers. We don't feel sorry for the bank itself. If you prick a bank it doesn't bleed. And let some years elapse and bank robbers can metamorphose into heroes. Ned Kelly now is Robin Hood. And Nick Leeson, who brought down the Barings Bank by speculating psychopathically, does not seem like a villain. A fool perhaps, a wild man sunk by greed, but not a villain.

Yet still, despite the grumbles and resentment, the mutterings of impotence, our comfort rests on banks. A run on the banks knocks struts from underneath our lives and makes us scared.

Banks are patriarchal figures, like serious remote Victorian fathers. We kick against them but we want them there. They underpin, they represent security.

Modern bankers understand all this. And in a bid to generate more business they strive to make us feel more warmth towards them. Their ads cry out for love. They paint themselves as donors of freedom. Come bank with us and you will paraglide to happiness. Come bank with us and you'll be stallion-free. Come bank with us and you will meet a very funny man.

But like advertisers everywhere they paint in bogus colours. Inside even the most open-plan and customer-friendly banks, the atmosphere is never playful, never funny, never free. It is austere and serious and churchlike. The queue is often silent as in church. Each customer goes to the counter as if to the confessional. Each conversation's private. And however much the teller-priest may smile and talk of weather or of sport, the conversation's nothing more than froth. Behind it, like the fat-doored safe behind the teller, there stands the iron-bound moral law of sums. And sins against that law are printed, as they've always been, in scarlet.

Yes, coach

Yesterday my toes curled and my voice went squeaky. I was just so excited. The world seemed fresh as dawn again. You see, I'd made a decision. I was going to change career. I was going to become a relationship coach.

To be honest, I'd only just learnt about the existence of relationship coaches. But as soon as I did, I knew I had to be one.

At Brighton Grammar School the careers adviser was a cheerful economics teacher. We never met. But if, in 1973, I had entered the economics room, parted my hair so that I could see, pulled up a chair and asked Mr Cheerful what he advised as a means of occupying, feeding, housing and clothing myself for the next half-century, he would have wheeled out traditional suggestions. 'Have you considered, Bennett,' he might have said, 'becoming a butcher, or a baker, or even, in these days of the OPEC oil crisis, a candlestick-maker?' But no mention of relationship coaches. Back then people were so absurdly self-reliant. They had boyfriends and girlfriends. Then they got married. Then they muddled through.

But now, despite the continuing existence of oil crises, we've grown up. We've found the courage to admit that we've become too sophisticated, that we've lost touch with the fundamentals.

Sex was the first to go. Our clever heads are so busy with clever things – text-messaging, virtual yachts, broccoli à la carbonara – that we've had to ditch stuff to make brain space. And what we've ditched are the instinctive bits. As a result we need help to do what no other animal needs help to do. The bookstores are crammed with sex manuals. And the Family Planning Association (is there a more dreary title in the world?) have rebranded themselves as 'sexperts' (yes, there is).

And that was only the start. Now we've admitted that it isn't just the coupling mechanics that are beyond us, whole relationships are. We need help. We need coaches. And yesterday I had it all worked out how to be one.

I would insist on being employed by both parties in any relationship. And I would concentrate on the early days, the budding of romance. Off to the restaurant I'd trot with the unhappy couple for a tête-à-tête-à-tête. I'd sit across the table with my don't-mind-me look and my tax-deductible grilled brill, eavesdropping, making notes, my mind abuzz, ready at any moment to take either client to one side.

'Stop,' I'd whisper to my man, 'your libido's showing. She knows all about your libido. The dreadful teen magazines she's been snuggling up with since she hit puberty at nine have told her all about your libido.'

'But,' he'd say.

'But me no buts,' I'd say, quoting merely to amuse myself, literature being as defunct as candlesticks, 'I'm the coach. And while I'm at it, stop boasting. She just doesn't care about your double overhead camshaft. Try letting her speak for once. You could even ask her a question. Oh, and ditch the aftershave. And that underarm stuff. Redundant, all of it. No deodorant will make her fancy you if she doesn't already. And if she does fancy you, you can turn up with an armpit full of skunks and she'll still be all over you.'

'But the ads . . .'

'Oh shut up and think for yourself,' I'd be about to say, but I'd bite my tongue because (a) the man was employing me, and (b) being unable to think for himself was the reason that he was employing me, and (c) it was time to address my other employer.

'Now come on, darling,' I'd say, inching my chair around the table, 'don't string him along. Yes, I know he's transparent as cellophane, but he just doesn't do complexity, all right? You can play emotional ping-pong with him as much as you like, but he'll keep missing the ball. Then he'll sulk. And if you insist on playing the ethereal angel bit, all eyelashes and mystery, well, on your own head be it. Of course, you'll soon have him panting like a dog in a heatwave, but for you there'll be no going back. Any hint after that of straightforward being-a-person stuff – you know, wanting your own way, or eating food, or going to the loo – and before you can say australopithecus he'll be flat out on the sofa grunting at the rugby. And please don't imagine that you'll change him. He's a bloke. You'll just make him furtive and sad.'

Doesn't that sound like fun? Well, it did to me. Yesterday. But now, this very morning, idling through the fatly barren Sunday paper, I found my toes curling and my voice squeaking at an even higher pitch than before. You see, I read about a profession that sounded more delightful still. And I'm going to take it up. I'm going to be a life coach.

'Breathe in,' I'll say to my client. 'Good, now breathe out. Excellent. Keep doing that. Well done. Now, smile if you can manage it, take a step forward and see what happens to happen.'

He was my English teacher

He's dead. Jack Smithies. My English teacher. Of cancer. I got an email today. Went off in his sleep. I've written about him before but I can't let his death pass without doing something. He was my English teacher.

I had other English teachers of course, but they didn't matter. They made no splash in my pond. There was one who got us to depict the legends of King Arthur in strip cartoons. In the seventies that sort of thing was in vogue. I couldn't see the point of it then and I can't now. Jack Smithies never did stuff that was in vogue.

After Mr Strip Cartoon came Ernie. Ernie was ancient and he taught me nothing. He took two years to do it. I can still recall the way Ernie spoke, as if someone had pulled his tongue a little bit too far forward and at the same time wedged something semi-permeable in the bridge of his nose. His was an easy voice to imitate. No one imitated Jack Smithies.

Ernie, bless him, made us parse sentences according to some strange scheme of his, but I never got it. I grasped the patterns of grammar only by doing foreign languages. Ernie also found Chaucer funny, or at least he made a point of explaining to us why Chaucer was funny, although Ernie himself never laughed at the jokes. Nor, as we spotted, did he explain the sex jokes. Then one fine day Andy Grant told Ernie that Chaucer wasn't funny. Ernie grew angry in a way I hadn't seen before. He was a placid beast but suddenly he was fury made flesh, bellowing at Andy and swinging his withered arms. Now *that* was funny. I don't recall Jack Smithies ever being angry.

Two years of Ernie must have meant a period a day for forty

weeks a year. That's 400 or so hours of teaching and nothing has stuck but his failures. Ah well. He tried. Rest his bones.

Further back still lie a string of primary teachers – women in tweed skirts, Miss Coghlin, Mrs Lake and one with warts. They did spelling tests, I suppose, and dreary foundation stuff, and I remember that Miss Coghlin cared about handwriting.

I always hated my handwriting. It said too much about me. I seemed unable to lie with it – not with the words I wrote, of course, they were always available to lie with – but with the way I shaped the letters. However much I tried to jazz my handwriting up with fancy Russian d's or capital F's written backwards like continental 7's, the shapes I made on the page still seemed to shout the immutable truths of my weakness of character. All the same, those women, those sturdy women teachers, they seemed good then and they still do now. But they didn't excite me. Jack Smithies did.

I did English at university. My director of studies was Nervous Tony, a distinguished medievalist, peeved not to be a professor, secretly sliding his laceless shoe on and off under the desk while telling me of Gawain and the Green Knight, pronounced 'kernikt', or reciting chunks of *Piers Plowman* from memory. No fun there. We didn't get on. I wrote a couple of bad short stories about him and his nervousness. I've written nothing but good things about Jack Smithies.

Nervous Tony farmed me out to a woman I liked. We still correspond. She came to my room for hours at a time, told me about her folk-singing husband, about growing tomatoes, about lesbians, about milk churns. She smoked my smokes, drank my coffee and was the first adult woman I ever saw as a real frail person. But though I liked her, I did little work for her.

After her I was deemed educated. They stamped my passport and let me loose. No English teachers since.

The ones I've noted didn't teach me much English. But then, once you've learnt to spell and punctuate there's not much left to learn. Or at least not much that can be taught.

And Jack, my English teacher, the one who counted, the one

who did make a splash in my pond, didn't teach me much either. No lapidary phrases, no moral precepts, no startling insights. He just showed me some writers, and showed that he liked them. It was Jack who introduced me to Larkin. But I'd have have found Larkin anyway.

So why did he matter? I don't know. Perhaps my mind just meshed with his. Anyway, he made me laugh. Not by telling jokes. Not by telling stories. But by, well, being Jack. He made a difference to me that I can't begin to define. It was largely because of him that I went on to study English. And it was largely because of him that I taught English for twenty years.

And now he's dead. Twenty-four hours dead. By the time you read this they'll have burned or buried him. Burned, I expect.

Hacksaw that shackle

Gloom? You can keep it. War, cloning, dingbat presidents, mini-golf, nuclear threats discussed by people who can't pronounce nuclear, Russell Crowe, wine-tastings, the road toll – they're all yours. I couldn't give a monkey's toolbox. This year's going to be just dandy for me. I'm bubbling. I'm rampant. I'm going to have a ball, a ball so big it will have its own weather system.

Why? Simple. I've made a resolution. I'm giving up fear. Just like that. The only puzzle is why I didn't do it before.

Of course, I'm not giving up primal fear. I'll remain scared of the real nasties. So when, say, I go to bed and see a spider on the ceiling I won't just be shutting the eyes and crossing the fingers. There remains a difference between fearlessness and foolishness. No, I'll still be fetching the vacuum cleaner and the extension wand, and I'll still wear rubber gloves to empty the dust bag, and I'll still put a brick on the lid of the bin just in case. So don't fret for my safety.

But all my social fears are going straight into history's bin alongside the spider. And so, at last, I shall put into practice the advice tendered by a vast Spanish drunk twenty-five years ago. He told me that there were three imperatives, and only three. As he enumerated them he jabbed me in the chest with a finger like a musket muzzle. And here is the prophet's recipe for living well.

'First,' he said, 'you must eat Serrano ham.'

'Si senor,' I said.

'And you must smoke Ducados,' he said.

'Absolutamente,' I said.

'And thirdly and finally,' he said, his brandy-rich voice rising to the pitch of a vicar who aims to wake the congregation for the sermon's moral climax, 'you must never be afraid of anything.'

So spake the godhead, and then, his duty done, he fell down and passed out of consciousness and my life. But though I didn't know it at the time, his message had lodged in my skull like a seed. And a quarter of a century later the seed has sprouted.

Admittedly Serrano ham tastes of boot leather, and Ducados cigarettes taste of graveclothes, and if you hold a Ducados with the tip pointing down the tobacco falls out, but it is clear to me now that parts one and two of the advice were mere preambles to the big part three.

Elsewhere I have written that advice is like aftershave: everyone likes to give it, but those who receive it don't use it. I do not retract those words. I am merely making a single exception and this is it. Never, from this day forth, the 1st of January 2003, shall I be afraid of anything.

For fear, you see, has been the shackle round the leg of my dreams. And now that I have taken the hacksaw to that shackle I shall blaze like a meteor across the great sky of possibility.

And the first fear to go will be my fear of people in authority.

Watch out, my darlings. Watch out, you jacks in office. Managers, bishops, chief executives, editors, tax inspectors, any of you, in short (and many of you are), who have a great big desk with too little on it, you have been warned. No more little Joe rolling over and dropping his kecks with a cry of 'Beat me harder. I deserve it, sir.' Oh no. Those days are gone. You'll be dealing henceforth with a man who has carborundum in his soul. And if I continue to make deals that seem soft to you, if I continue to behave like a craven worm, a worm you can trample on your way to the top, be aware that you are being fooled. I shall be conceding only out of pity, pity for you. Got it? Good.

And as for the rest of you, well you won't be spared either. Because my next fear to go is the fear of giving offence. Henceforth I shall give offence by the kilometre. I shall be so offensive I'll be harried by the obscenity squad. But I won't care. They won't frighten me any more. And nor will you.

Nor shall I ever again be afraid of what other people might think of me. If you don't believe me, try coming within a 50-yard radius of my new-found fearlessness and using the word 'spirituality'. You just try it. Or try telling me about Tuscany, or praising margarine, or getting me to read your poetry. Never will you have heard the phrase 'Well, that's interesting' spoken with such undiluted venom. And if you still don't understand what 'interesting' means, well, you're beyond redemption.

Bores, you've had it. You're road-kill. 'I hope I'm not boring you,' you'll say, to which the new and fearless me will reply, 'Yes, you bloody well are.' For sure I may laugh afterwards and say, 'No, really, just joking, do go on', but you'll have heard. You'll know. The serpent of fearless honesty will have nipped your heart.

Oh, I'll have such fun in 2003. Gloom? You can keep it. I do hope you don't mind.

Hot wet air

From the twenty-first floor of the Excelsior Hotel I can see the mouth of the Singapore River. Beyond it in the open sea a massive fleet of cargo ships lies at anchor. This place was built on trade.

Near the water's edge a group of boys plays soccer. I don't know how they can. Singapore sits smack on the equator. The air's like a wet oven.

To one side stands the spire of the Cathedral of St Andrew. I went there yesterday. The place had all the bits that make a Western church – vaulted ceiling, stone columns, brass eagle lectern, font and organ, pew backs crammed with hymnbooks – but it was hot. The twenty hanging electric fans did nothing but stir the heat. Seated on a wickerwork pew I felt no relief from the city. My trousers were sodden at the crotch. Skin stuck to cloth, to skin. There was hot wet grit in my armpits, in the creases of my neck.

The church seemed like what it is, a transplant from the cool north, ill-suited to the globe's sweltering girdle. High up on the west wall of the church, something jungle-luxuriant sprouted from the spouting. You could see it getting bigger.

The church doesn't fit here. Nor do white people. We are too lardy and large. In the hotel lobby, Australian women in late middle age with truck-tyre waists and bangled flabby arms are loud and crass. I wince at our shared heritage. And yet Singapore is endlessly polite to us. It takes our bags and pampers us with yes-sir, no-sir. The air-conditioning and courtesy invite us just to spend.

Two centuries ago it was not so. Up empty Canning Rise there is an imitation of a European park. The grass is coarse and broad of leaf and the soil is sand, but there are band rotundas and benches under trees, and there I found the tombstones of some European dead. In 1863 a sailor born in Telpham, Sussex, died aged twenty-one. The tropics took him, raddled him no doubt with some extravagant disease that blew him up or shrank him, turned his young flesh purple, shook his teeth out, killed him. His shipmates all chipped in to build his tomb. The tropics got that too. The tomb caved in. Only the headstone survived to be bricked into a wall.

Nearby stands the Wesleyan church. An information board boasts the evangelical history of the place. Hot wet air has crept behind the glass to make most of the boast illegible.

Some fifty cranes are clustered on a building site. Signs announce the construction of the Singapore Institute of Management, with posters of happy students doing handstands. The workmen on the site are skinny, muscled and dark, their chocolate eyes set deep in the head. I can only guess at their race. This is a city of many races. There are tiny Chinese girls, turbaned Sikhs, broad-faced Malays and probably a hundred other Asian races I can't discriminate. If there is an indigenous population, I don't know what it is. And the heat makes me incurious.

As everybody knows, Singapore is orderly. There is no chewing gum. Nor, in the centre of the city at least, are there beggars or litter. Those who would be begging are employed to sweep the streets. Each carries a worn broom and a plastic pan on a stick.

The hand of authority lies heavily on the place. Inside the buildings a hundred thousand signs say 'No Smoking – By Law'. Unnecessary security guards stand sentry outside shops and hotels. No hawkers pester me. Everyone obeys the pedestrian lights. A blinking numeral counts down the seconds left to me to cross the road. I take them all.

Shopping malls abound, cool and multi-storeyed, neon-lit and primary-coloured, open late into the night. In Raffles City Shopping Plaza there is Marks & Spencer, and Aunt Jodie's coffee bar. The ground floor holds a temporary exhibition of Australian produce. Yesterday, among the people picking over merino woollen clothes, boxed Tasmanian honeycombs and glassware painted by authentic Aborigines, were quite a few Australians.

In the Raffles City Shopping Plaza Food Mart I drank a mango smoothie and ate five dollars worth of noodles topped with duck. The duck was mostly bone. To smoke I had to go outside. On a low wall by a carpark I sat and wrote some notes. The ballpoint ink took time to dry. The moisture had nowhere to go. Under a hedge trimmed military square a fat rat nosed for rubbish and found none.

This morning, with time to kill before my taxi to the airport, I make a final sortie out into the heat. In the hotel forecourt I ask a man in uniform to tell me somewhere good for breakfast.

'Madonna,' he says, and points along the street.

'Madonna?'

'Madonna,' he repeats and smiles. 'Good,' he says. 'American.'

I cotton on and smile back. 'No,' I say, 'not McDonald's. Is there somewhere more, well, more Singaporean?'

'Singaporean?' he says.

I nod. He smiles and shrugs.

I thank him and trudge away. My feet are swollen. It's not the place's fault, but I'll be pleased to leave. I don't belong.

A coupette

I am tempted to seize power. I won't bother with an election. Elections give the top job to someone who's joined a political party, and what we don't need in the nation's cockpit is the sort of person that joins a political party. Such people can be spotted as third formers – it's already there in their pencil cases, their socks, the mudguards on their bicycles. They're too keen.

So, no election for me. Just a cheerful stroll down Lambton Quay, up the grey stone steps, a dismissive wave to security in its perspex booth and appalling uniform – oh, how Wellington loves a uniform; like all capital cities it's just a swollen prefects' common room – then up to the ninth floor. The eviction dialogue will be brief. 'Sorry dearie,' I'll say with a smile mixing feigned sympathy and unfeigned authority, 'but the time has come. Gather all those lovely mementoes of your time in office – the handwritten letter from Bush (don't they teach joined-up writing any more?), the signed first edition of *John Howard's Collected Wit and Wisdom*, that gift from the Saudi prince of a hip flask got up to look like the Koran – and off you toddle. No dear, you don't seem to understand, the will of the people doesn't come into it. This is something altogether less airbrushed, honeybun. This is what we in the trade call a coup.'

Or, to be frank, a coupette. Because, you see, I don't plan to hang on to the job for long. A fortnight should do it. Knowing myself to be a frail and mortal beast I am aware that I would succumb to the same temptations as they all succumb to. Give me a month in office and I'd be knocking up laws banning things. Of course I'd be banning the things that needed banning – grief counsellors, the Consumers Institute, obsequious excitement at the presence on these shores of a Hollywood starlet, anchovies – but more laws, however virtuous, are not what we need. We need fewer laws. So I'll spend my first thirteen days in office abolishing every law that suggests we can't look after ourselves. The swimming pool fence stuff, the food-label stuff – you can make your own list.

And then on the last day of my reign, with a fanfare and a mass rally choreographed to Piaf's 'Milord', I'll announce one new law. It will consist of a single clause. The clause will be followed by an appendix detailing the penalties for transgression.

The clause: You shall say what you mean.

The appendix: Or else.

And bang, at a stroke I shall outlaw PR English, officialese, the smokescreen language of bureaucracy. I've been railing against these things for years and a fat lot of good it's done. So now, action.

Recently a woman wrote to the paper to complain that when her family took four cans of L&P to a one-day international cricket match, security confiscated those cans. She wanted to know why. Here's the reply.

'To ensure the health and safety of customers at all Jade Stadium events is not compromised, stadium policy prohibits any can being brought into the venue.

'Unfortunately a can, regardless of its contents, is generally regarded as a potentially dangerous object in the sporting venue environment and for that reason is not permitted in most major New Zealand stadiums.'

Under my new law the author of this stuff will be in court before you can say rubber truncheon. The court transcript will read as follows. (Did I mention that I was going to sit on the bench as well? Well I am. I'm going to sit on it so hard it will snap.)

Me: So, 'stadium policy prohibits', does it?

Defendant: Yes, your honour.

Me: And who, pray, wrote the stadium policy?

Defendant: We did, your honour.

Me: But you didn't say so, did you? And you went on to use the passive form of the verb to sound authoritative while evading responsibility, didn't you?

Defendant (abjectly hanging head): I did, your honour.

Me: Because if 'a can is generally regarded as a potentially dangerous object', who does the regarding?

Defendant: I am overcome with a sense of guilt at my use of the evasive passive, your honour.

Me: Silence. I've only just started to have fun.

Defendant: Please don't draw everyone's attention to the absurdity of the word 'health', your honour, nor to the notion of it being 'compromised', nor to the appalling phrase 'sporting venue environment'. I see where I went wrong. I just meant that some people throw cans.

Me: But you didn't say so, did you? I hereby sentence you to the only penalty which the law allows, 'or else'.

Defendant (blanching): You mean?

Me: Yes. I sentence you to a terribly long time in the slammer where you can inform your fellow inmates that 'approaches of an aggressive or intimate nature are generally regarded as unacceptable and liable to compromise the health and safety of other inmates in a corrective facility environment' and see how you get on. Take him down.

At which point I shall return to the life of a dog-walking hermit confident that I have made the world a better place and equally confident that somebody else will bugger it up again soon.

Easter rising

Easter Sunday, Hitler's birthday, mine too, as it happens, and this morning saw the resurrection of Grandma Chook, which is as good a birthday present as I've had since the pair of handcuffs. To be frank, Grandma Chook wasn't actually dead, but I thought she was, which if you think about it, and I did, is worse. I mean, if you're not dead but people think you are, and they're rootling in the cupboard for something to wear to your funeral and a few words to say about you that aren't actively malicious, it's no time to pop back up saying, 'Yoohoo, it's me, yes, that's right, I was just foxing, God what a horrible suit.' No, you're better off out of it.

Which is what I thought Grandma Chook was, only I couldn't find the corpse. She disappeared on whatever they call the day before Good Friday – Okay Thursday, perhaps – and no hint of her since.

She was a callous old matriarch, much given to bullying the other chooks, all of whom are her daughters or granddaughters. Having ruled the roost for half a decade she had grown monstrously fat, far too fat to even think of flying, too fat indeed to hop up a 1-foot retaining wall that I built and which is still, remarkably, retaining. So fat was Grandma Chook that whenever I appeared at the back door and she came barrelling down the slope with her greed and fluffy underskirts to ensure she was first to bury her beak in the trough, gravity regularly took her a couple of yards past the target and dumped her in a feathery heap against the fence with her multiple offspring all trying hard not to giggle.

But then, suddenly, on Okay Thursday, there she was, gone. I checked her usual roosting sites, I checked the nesting box where she retires twice a year to brood, I fossicked through the under-growth like a police search party of one, but zilch, zip, nothing, only a hole where she'd been. And to my surprise I missed her. I missed her bossy clucking selfish vigour, and it didn't make for a very Good Friday. Nor, for that matter, a Super Saturday, especially when added to the antics of the Post Office.

Did you get one of those billets doux from New Zealand Post? Dear Householder and Victim, it said, we've decided to give our coochy-coo postie-wosties an extra day off on Super Saturday so they can have a really jolly time at Easter with their kiddiwinkies and you can have virtually a whole week without mail. Please use this card to tell us whether you think this is a good idea, even though we're going to do it anyway, or whether you think we should keep our postie-wosties working every hour that God gives until they are skeletal husks fit only for paupers' graves.

Naturally I wrote back. Whip 'em to death, I wrote, in red ink and capital letters, but it won't make any difference. Not that it matters, I suppose, since no one writes letters any more and all the postie ever brings me is illiteracies from real estatists, and su-permarket fliers telling me how cheaply I can buy a dead chook, which, frankly, was not what I needed right then.

What I needed right then on Super Saturday, with a pall of gloom, loss and solitude descending, was available at the Lava Bar for four dollars a pint. Down the evening hill I toddled with the slightly less than full moon squatting above the plantation ridge like a giant egg. Never – and when I say never, I mean not all that often – have I seen the moon looking more egglike, which, as I said straight off to the barman, was singularly apt for Easter. That, inevitably, led to a grand discussion of the etymology of the word Easter, which I said went back to some pagan festival called Oestre that the church hijacked, as is its habit, and the barman said was it related to oestrogen, that being something to do with eggs and fertility, to which I said with resonant conviction that I hadn't got a clue. I went on to lament the fate of Grandma Chook and everyone said how sad they were, which was about as convincing as a party political broadcast, and then the evening ended in the not so small hours in a bizarre escapade with someone else's dog which was jolly while it lasted.

So ten seconds or so after waking on Easter Sunday I realised I was unwell and forty-six for the first time in my life. I stumbled out to feed the chooks and from under the house there came a huffing and a clucking and a flapping of elderly wings and out waddled Grandma Chook. She was famished. I watched her eat a bushel or two of grain and then followed her back under the house where somehow she had amassed a clutch of twenty eggs, all of them infertile, which she was spending her Easter holidays trying to hatch. And as I reached under her to remove the eggs – because if I didn't she would sit on them till Easter next – she pecked my hand with what I can only describe as undisguised and entirely typical malice. Welcome back from the dead, I said, and I meant it.